HARMONY NOTES

HARMONY NOTES

BOOK 2

JEAN ARCHIBALD and MARIE MORAN

Carysfort Press

RIAM
Royal Irish Academy of Music

PETER LANG
Lausanne • Berlin • Bruxelles • Chennai • New York • Oxford

Bibliographic information published by The German National Library.
Die Deutsche Nationalbibliothek lists this publication in the German National Bibliography; detailed bibliographic data is available on the Internet at http://dnb.d-nb.de.

A catalogue record for this book is available from the British Library.

Library of Congress Control Number: 2021025137.

The audio examples and download exercises contained in this book can be accessed from the Peter Lang website <https://doi.org/10.3726/b21154> under the heading of 'Resources to supplement Harmony Notes book 2'.

Cover image designed by Gareth Teggin.

Cover design by Brian Melville for Peter Lang Ltd.

ISBN 978-1-80079-648-5 (print)
ISBN 978-1-80374-182-6 (ePDF)
ISBN 978-1-80374-183-3 (ePub)
DOI 10.3726/b21154

Published by Peter Lang Ltd, Oxford, United Kingdom
info@peterlang.com - www.peterlang.com

This publication has been peer reviewed.

TABLE OF CONTENTS

Preface

This book is the second in a two-part series addressing the fundamentals in the study and teaching of tonal music harmony.
Whilst *Harmony Notes: Book 1,* provides an introduction to vocal harmony, *Harmony Notes: Book 2* expands via a carefully graded sequence of material encompassing dissonant decoration, modulation, secondary 7^{ths} and an exploration of Classical chromatic harmony.

The 17 chapters of Book 2 follow the format and layout as that used in *Harmony Notes: Book 1*. There are a number of threads at the core of the design and layout which run consistently throughout all chapters:

- Central to the ethos of the project and as a way of elucidating information, the principle of 'sound and symbol' is at the core. Aural examples support the introduction of every new concept, underpinning the sound.
- New vocabulary is explored in context followed by clear uncomplicated explanations and worked examples – with the learner always in mind.
- Exercises are carefully graded and follow the delivery of new material; thus creating a 'workbook' angle within the body of the text.
- Significant grammatical nuggets are flagged by 'lightbulb' icons. Salient points are highlighted in 'checklist' and 'summary' boxes, while all audio examples are indicated by interactive 'headphone' logos.

To broaden the scope a little beyond four-part vocal harmony, the study of short extracts from piano and string quartet literature are included, thus enabling the student to hear, recognise and appreciate learnt progressions in a wider context.

Whilst there is a necessary emphasis on the grammatical detail, a creative musical approach is always encouraged.

All audio material will be made available on the Web to accompany the text. The exercises are embedded in the text and are also available as downloads for ease of completion and correction.

We hope that this book provides the student with a solid understanding and skill set in approaching Baroque and Classical 4-part harmony. We endeavour to foster a curiosity to explore the rich tapestry of harmonic language in different periods and genres.

Acknowledgements

We would like to thank many people and in particular Deborah Kelleher, Director of the Royal Irish Academy of Music whose fulsome support, encouragement and enthusiasm was unwavering throughout the entire life of this project.

We are indebted to our loyal friends and colleagues for their ongoing support and encouragement in completing the project.

We would like to extend a special thanks to Gareth Teggin for creating the cover image and designing the 'headphone' logo for the audio tracks. His generous advice and expertise in teasing out technical issues has been invaluable at all stages throughout the project.

We appreciate the valuable advice given by Jonathan Nangle in processing the audio examples.

Philip Shields, librarian in the RIAM deserves a special mention for his guidance and direction at various stages of the project.

Finally, we would like to thank Dr. Dan Farrelly of Carysfort Press, Dublin and Peter Lang Ltd. (International Academic Publishers), for undertaking this publication.

CHAPTER 1

SUSPENSIONS

Suspensions are a form of dissonant decoration and are extremely effective in creating tension and release in the harmonic writing. The effect of a suspension is to create a dissonance by delaying a chord note; the dissonance then resolves to the delayed chord note (consonance), giving the music a sense of forward movement.

Audio 1.1

Listen to the various extracts from a number of Bach chorales where the suspension decoration is highlighted.

Als der gutige Gott

O Haupt voll Blut und Wunden

Wo soll ich fliehen hin

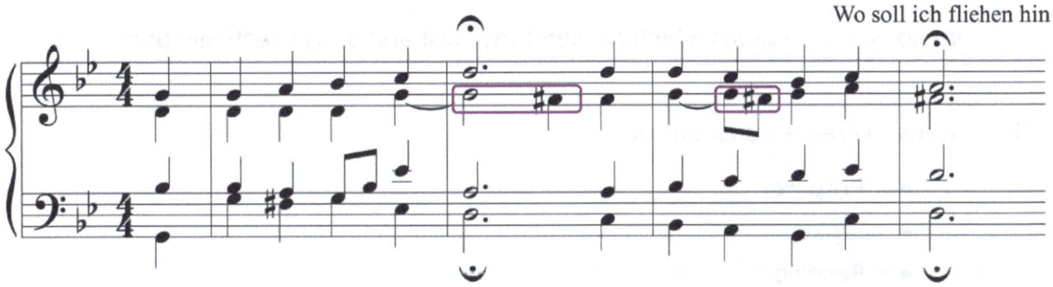

Suspensions on root position chords

To begin, suspensions will be used on root position chords delaying the root or 3rd in the upper voices. The chord note is delayed by the note one step above.

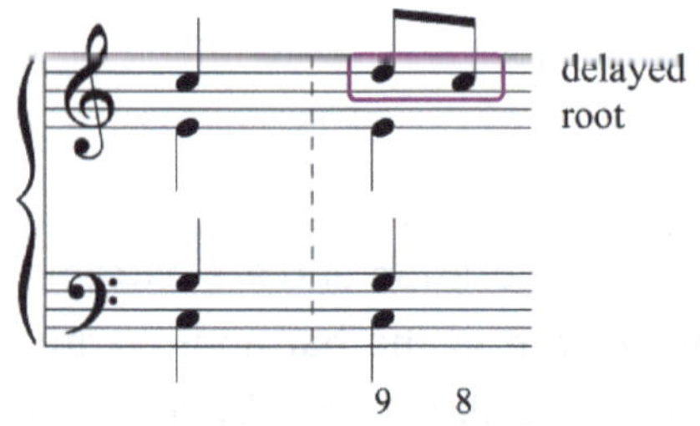

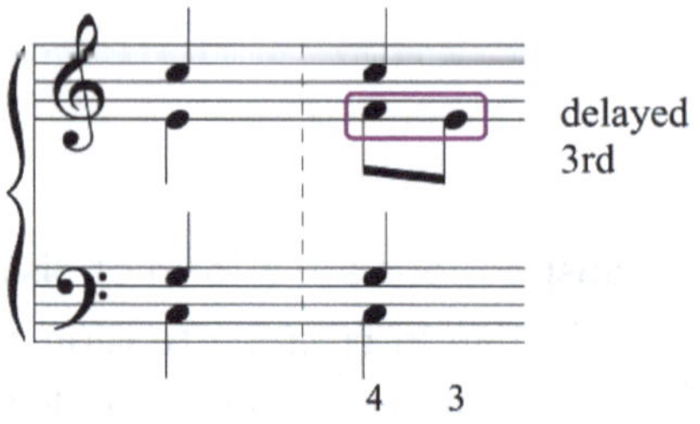

It is common practice to indicate the dissonant decoration in the figured bass.

Prepare

To complete the shape of a suspension, the dissonant note must be prepared by appearing as a **harmony** note in the previous chord in the same voice part.

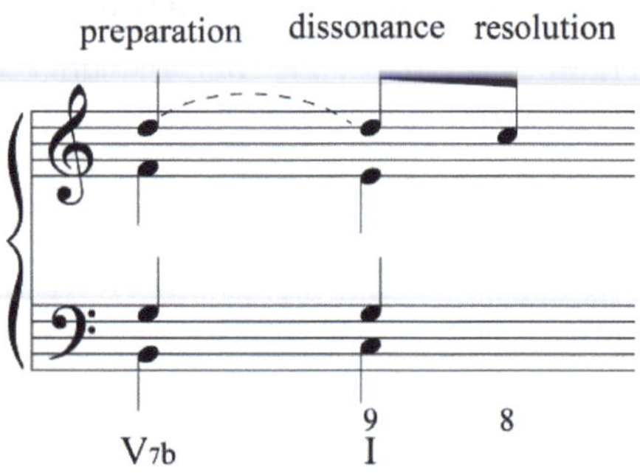

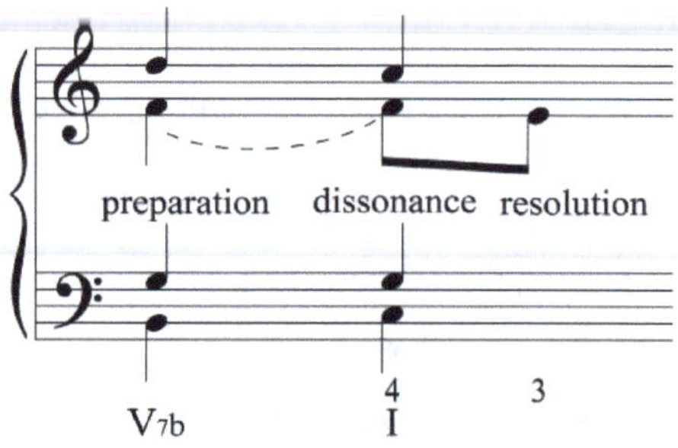

Strike

The dissonant note, which causes the tension, must occur on a strong beat or a strong part of any beat i.e., it must be accented. It is commonly tied; it may also be restruck.

Resolve

The dissonant note releases the tension as it resolves down a step to the harmony note it displaces.

Audio 1.2

Listen to the two previous progressions which suspend the root and 3rd respectively of chord **I**.

Three steps to create a suspension

- Prepare
- Strike
- Resolve

Rhythmic layout

The suspension/dissonance must be accented. Various rhythmic possibilities are shown below.

On the accented beat

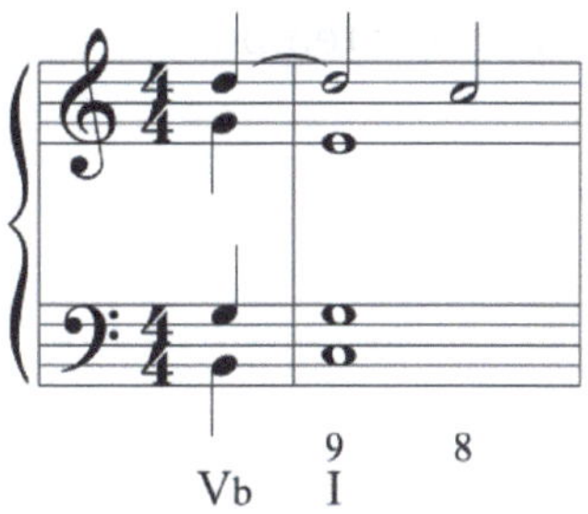

Audio 1.3

Listen to the first example from above.

On the accented part of a beat

(a)

(b)

(c)

(d)

Audio 1.4

Listen to each of the progressions above noting the rhythmic placement of the suspensions.

In all the examples so far notice that the resolution note is never longer than the dissonant note. However, in a slow triple tempo, the following is also a possibility in order to create a stronger sense of phrase ending.

This rhythm is more likely at a cadence in a slower tempo.

Audio 1.5

Listen to the above suspensions noting the sense of closure achieved.

An important consideration . . .

In order that the suspension be most effective, do not anticipate its resolution in another **upper** voice. This detracts from the tension and release effect. However, it is possible for the resolution note to be already in the **bass** voice.

Here the resolution is already in the tenor voice which spoils the effect of the suspension in the soprano.

In the corrected version the resolution is already in the **bass** voice. This is the only voice part that can duplicate the resolution.

Take care not to strike the suspension and resolution **together** in an upper voice

Audio 1.6

Listen to the major key examples below and study the movement of each suspension.

Audio 1.7

Study the following minor key examples taking note of the figured bass.

Remember that an accidental sign without a number directly beside it, always refers to the 3rd above the bass.

Exercise 1.1

Continue to add figured bass at the appropriate points to indicate the movement of the 9 – 8 and 4 – 3 suspensions. The first suspension in each case is figured for you.

(a)

(b)

Exercise 1.2

(a) Rewrite the following progressions to include a 4 – 3 suspension in the appropriate voice part.

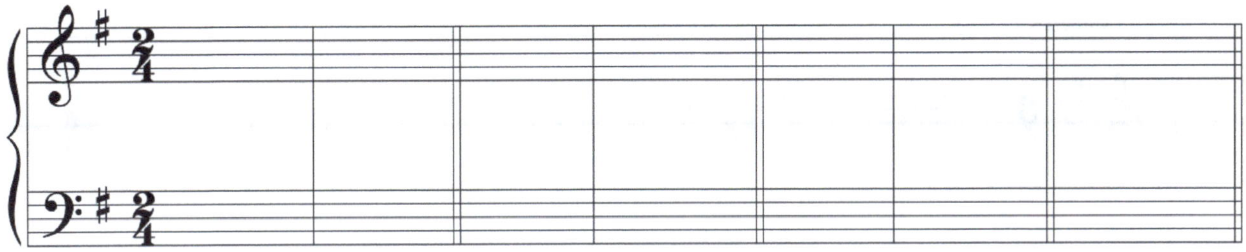

(b) Rewrite the following progressions to include a 9 – 8 suspension in the appropriate voice part.

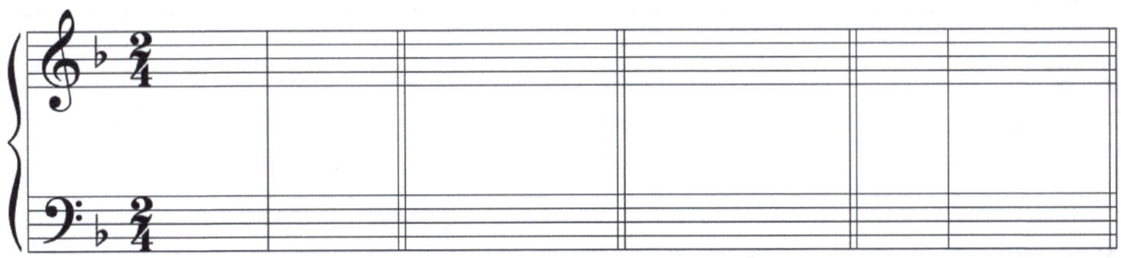

Exercise 1.3

Study the given passages adding roman numerals. Then rewrite each to include examples of 4 – 3 and 9 – 8 suspensions in any appropriate upper voice part. Include figured bass.

(a)

Numerals ______________________________

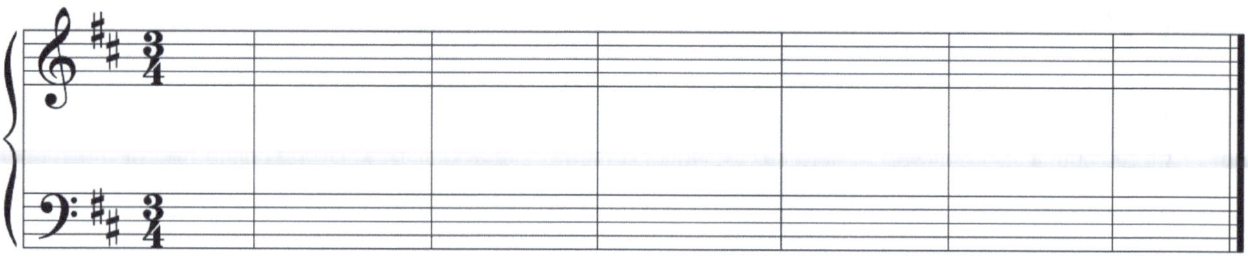

(b)

Numerals ______________________________

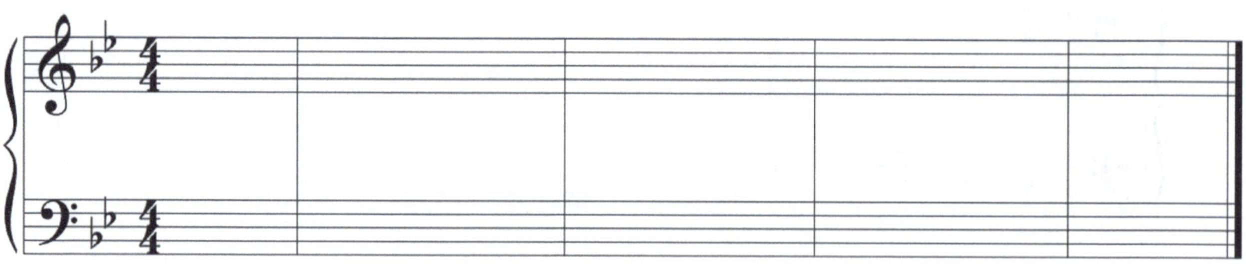

Exercise 1.4

Complete the harmony by adding alto and tenor parts. Follow the given figured bass. Add roman numerals in b and c.

(a)

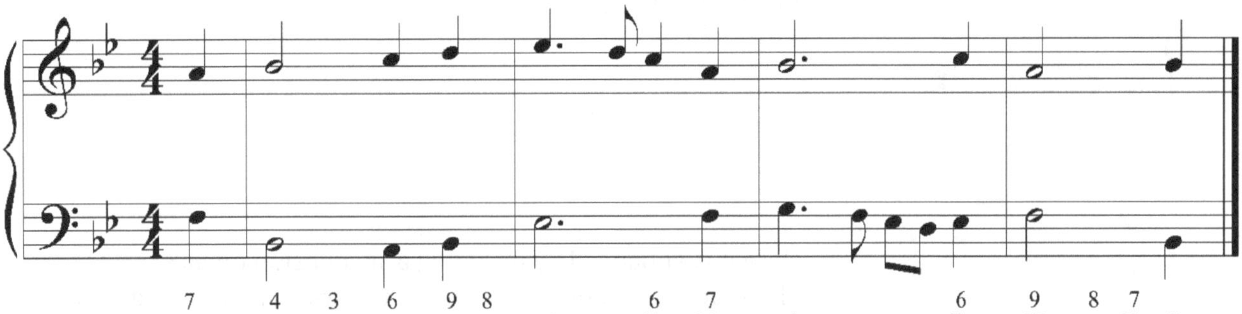

(b)

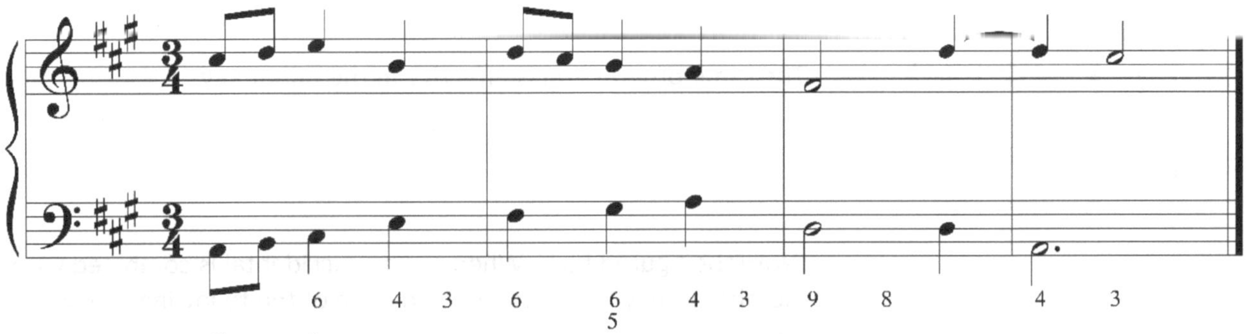

(c)

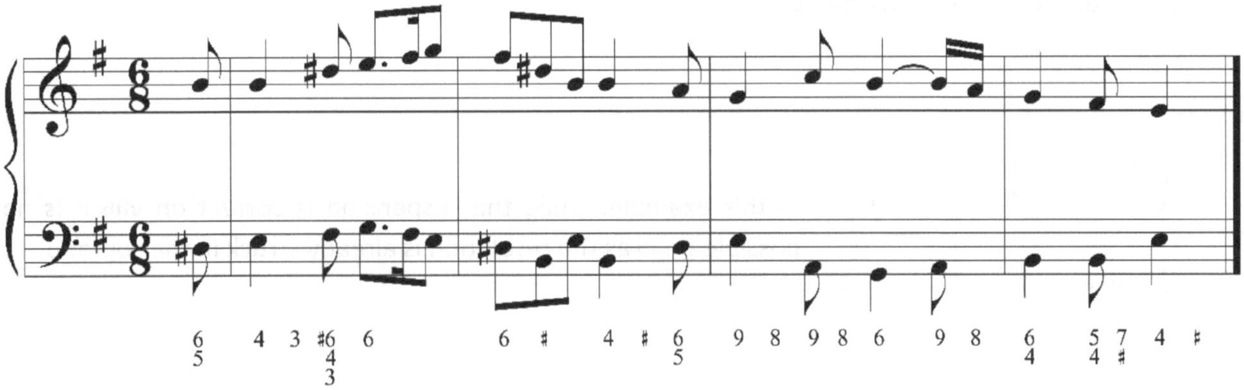

Numerals ______________________________

Suspensions on first inversion chords

A suspension on a first inversion chord will delay the **root** in an upper voice.

Remember this progression?

Here it is enhanced by including a suspension on **viib.**
The suspension delays the root in the soprano and is figured 7 – 6.

The same progression is effective in the minor key.

Note the figured bass. When a sharp accidental is combined with a number it may be indicated in any one of the following 3 ways:

♯6 6♯ 6̶

Audio 1.8

Listen to the progressions above.

In this example, while the suspension is correct on **viib** it is not possible on **Ib** as the resolution is already struck in the soprano.

In this example different doubling is used in the alto (5th), to avoid anticipating the resolution in the tenor and therefore give an effective suspension.

Audio 1.9

Listen to the second correct version above.

Exercise 1.5

Add figured bass at the appropriate points to indicate the movement of the 7 – 6 suspension.

Here is a worked example in F major first showing a harmonisation without suspensions. It is then rewritten to include various suspensions. Study both carefully.

Audio 1.10

Now listen and compare both versions noticing the added interest created by the suspensions.

Exercise 1.6

Decorate the harmony by rewriting to include 7 – 6 and 4 – 3 suspensions as appropriate in any of the upper voices.

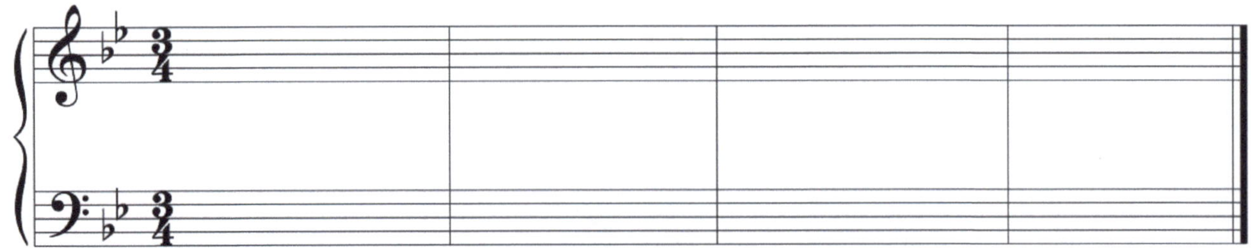

Exercise 1.7

Complete parts for soprano, alto and tenor voices carefully incorporating the suspension decoration as indicated by the figuring. Include roman numerals.

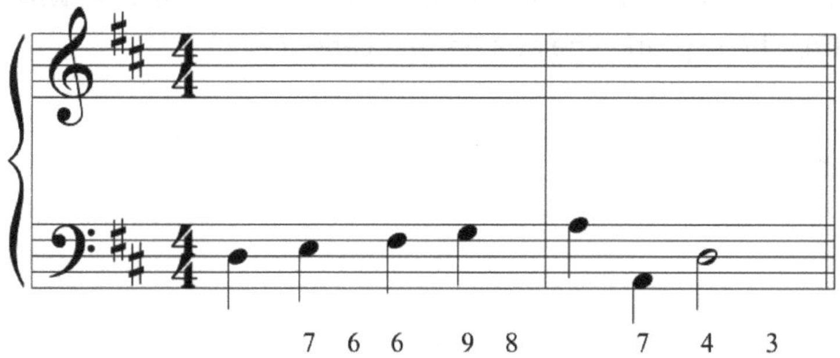

Numerals ____

Numerals ____

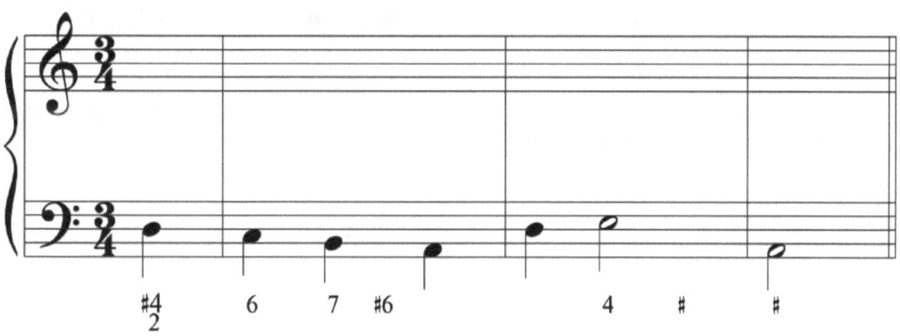

Numerals ____

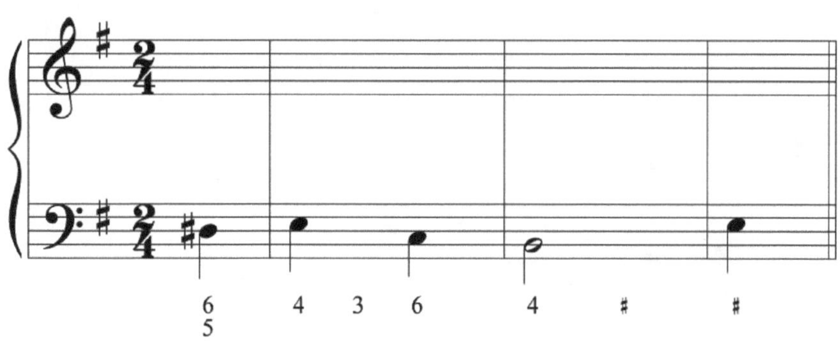

Numerals ____

Suspension involving the leading note

Here is an example of a suspension commonly used which successfully resolves upwards – this is the leading note delaying the arrival of the tonic. This suspension is most effective when decorating the soprano line at a perfect cadence.

Audio 1.11

Listen to the effect of the 7 – 8 suspension in both major and minor keys.

Double suspensions

It is often effective to have suspensions in two upper voices delaying the root and 3rd of the chord simultaneously. This enriches and softens the harmonic effect. Some of the most satisfactory combinations are: 7 – 8 and 4 – 3, also 9 – 8 and 4 – 3.

Audio 1.12

Listen carefully as you study the major key examples below.

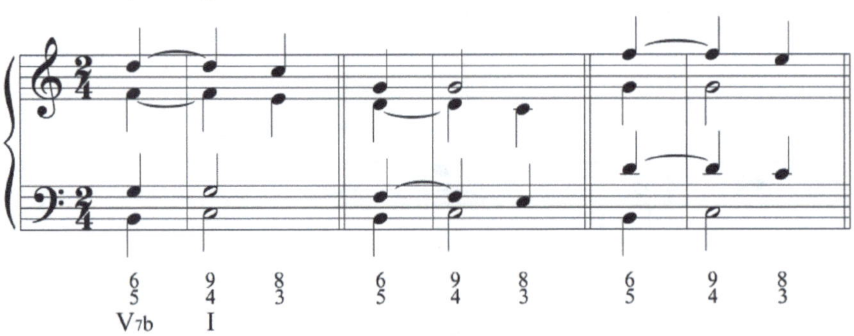

In a single suspension the leading note to the tonic is best in the soprano line. In a double suspension the leading note to the tonic may be in any upper voice.

Audio 1.13

Listen to these minor key examples.

Remember that the figures in a figured bass are listed in descending order regardless of their placement in the various voices.

Exercise 1.8

Study the exercises below adding roman numerals. Then rewrite each to include single and double suspensions in any of the upper voices. Include figured bass.

(a)

Numerals ____________________

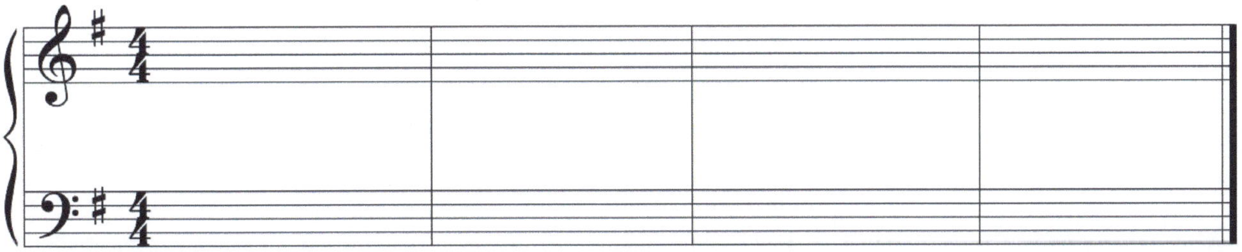

(b)

Numerals

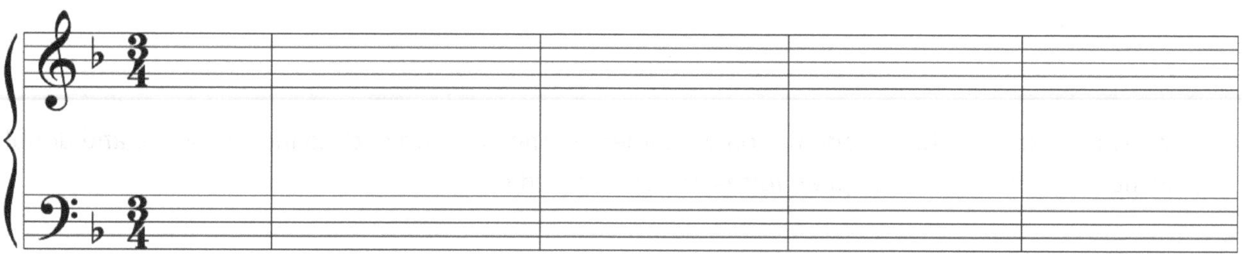

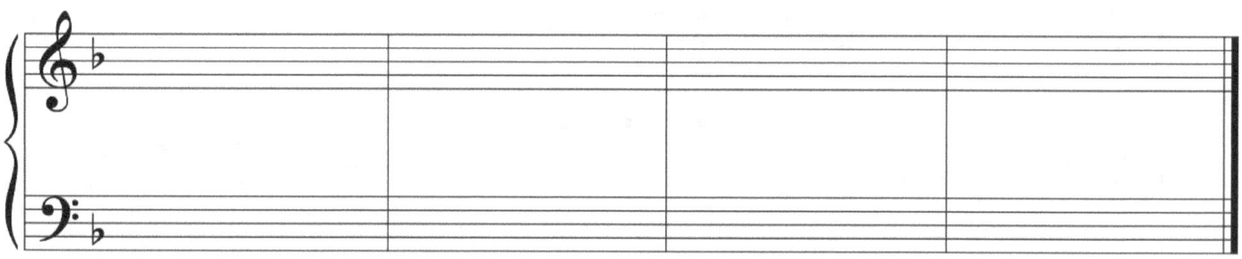

Exercise 1.9

Complete the harmony by adding alto and tenor parts following the figured bass. Add roman numerals.

(a)

Numerals ______________________________

(b)

Numerals ______________________________

____

Triple suspensions

Occasionally a final perfect cadence may be decorated with a triple suspension in the upper voices. This prolongs the release into the final chord. For this to be successful the final tonic chord must have a tripled root.

(a)

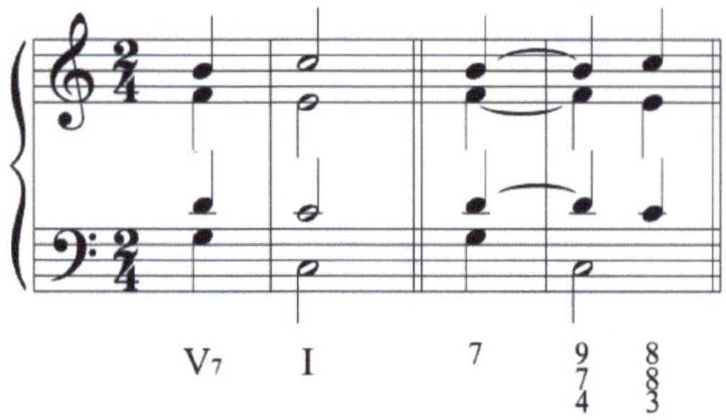

(b)

(c)

(d)

Audio 1.14

You will first hear each basic cadence above followed by its decorated form.

Exercise 1.10

Complete these decorated cadential progressions following the figured bass.

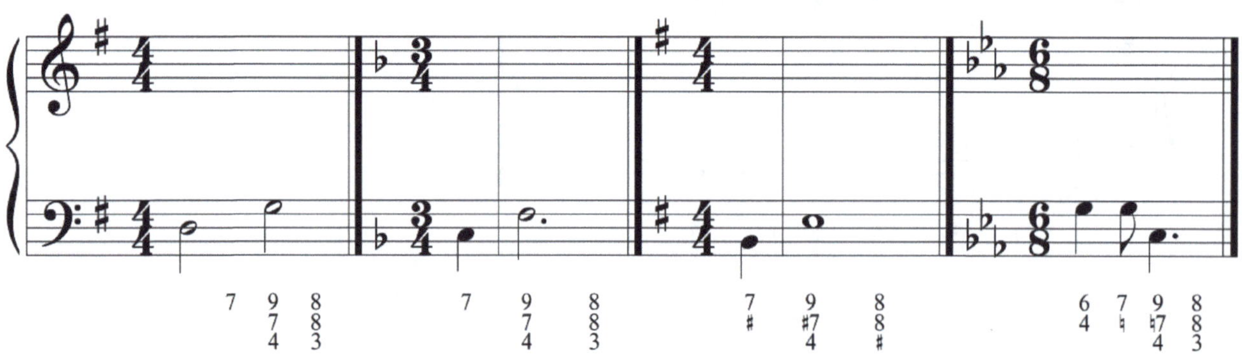

Bass suspension

Suspensions in the bass are used less frequently. Care must be taken not to muddy the intended harmony. At present, the bass suspension will be limited to delaying the 3rd of a chord (i.e., the bass of a first inversion). Here are some examples to listen to and study.

Audio 1.15

The plain progression is heard first followed by the suspended bass.

Notice that the bass suspension will **always** resolve downwards.

Notice that the bass suspension is **always** used alone.

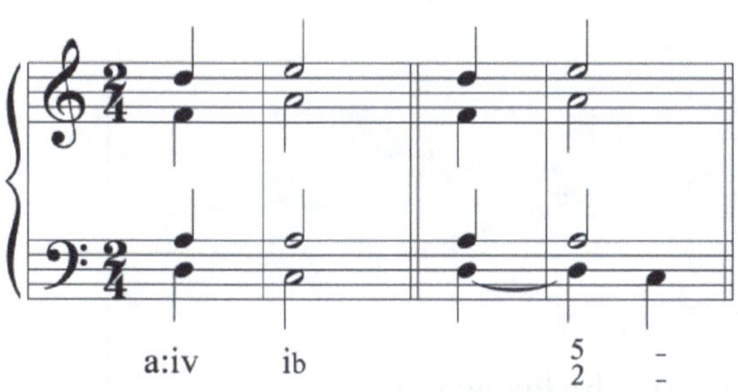

Notice the figured bass. The numbers are **always** calculated from the printed bass note. The two extended lines following the numbers indicate the sustained upper parts while the bass resolves the dissonance.

Exercise 1.11

Complete the missing voices as appropriate according to the figured bass. Add roman numerals.

Numerals ______________________________

Numerals ______________________________

Before approaching the next group of exercises study this summary of the main points in relation to suspensions.

Summary

- Target the root or 3rd of any chord
- The 3 steps are: prepare, strike, resolve
- The dissonance must be accented
- All dissonances resolve downwards except for the leading note
- The resolution must not be struck with the dissonance in any upper part
- Single, double, and triple suspensions are possible
- Bass suspensions must be used alone

Exercise 1.12

Complete the harmonisation by adding alto and tenor parts according to the figured bass. Add roman numerals.

(a)

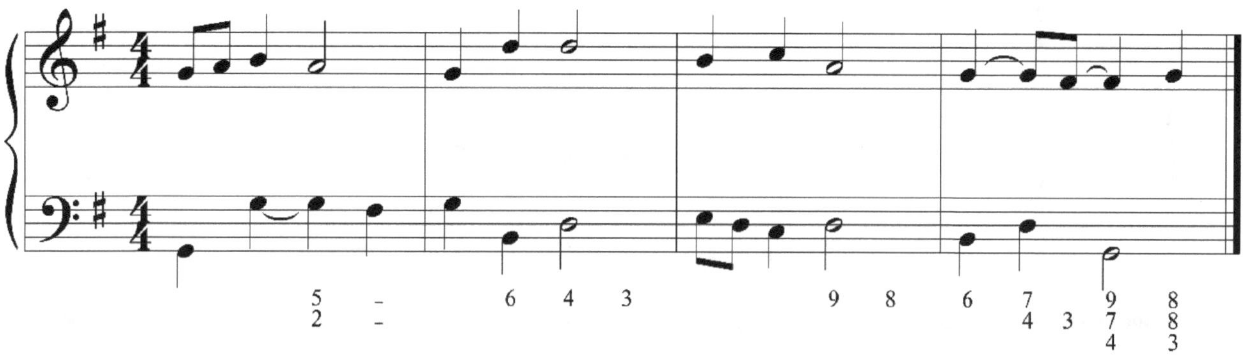

Numerals ____________________

(b)

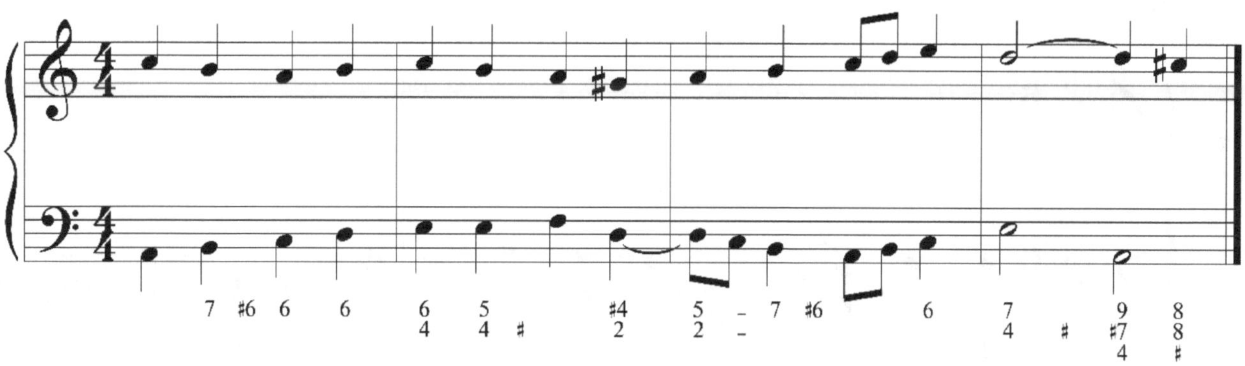

Numerals ____________________

Exercise 1.13

Complete the harmonisation by adding soprano, alto and tenor parts. Always craft the soprano line first. Include roman numerals.

(a)

Numerals ____

(b)

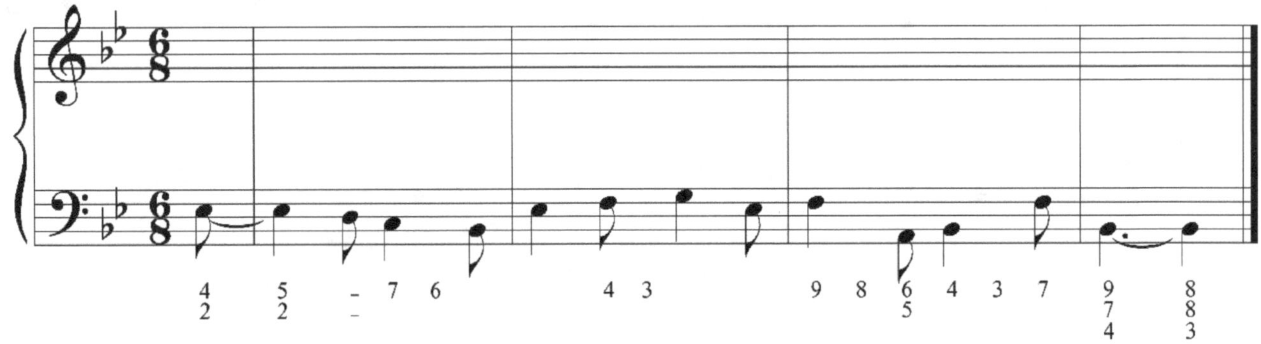

Numerals ____

Exercise 1.14

(a) Harmonise the given soprano melody in G minor. Begin by writing the complete bass line. Then add alto and tenor parts. Consider whether additional suspensions are appropriate in any of the added voices. Include roman numerals.

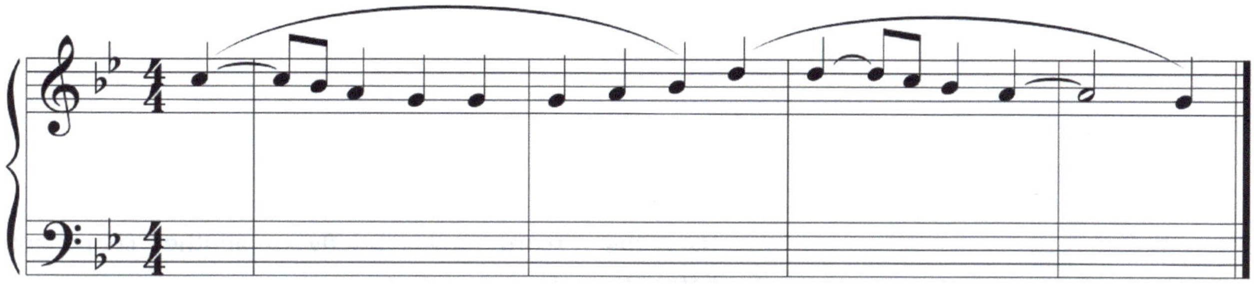

Numerals ____

(b) Harmonise the given soprano melody. Begin by writing the complete bass line. Then add alto and tenor parts. Consider whether additional suspensions are appropriate in any of the added voices. Include figured bass.

A little extra!

Occasionally, for added interest, a suspension can be ornamentally resolved. This is most likely to occur approaching a cadential point.

This progression shows the suspension with a normal resolution.

Here the discord moves briefly to another chord note before the actual resolution.

In this example the discord moves to the note one step below the resolution before finally resolving.

A further enhancement to the previous example is to fill the gap with a passing note, creating an attractive stepwise shape.

Note that in all cases, the final resolution note falls on the expected beat.

Audio 1.16

First you hear the suspension with a normal resolution, then the same suspension followed by various ornamental resolutions.

Audio 1.17

In this extract from the madrigal *'Come again, sweet love'* by John Dowland, you will hear the suspension ornamentally resolved in the context of its final cadence.

One further consideration!

In most cases the harmony remains static while the suspension resolves. However, two other possibilities may arise; (i) the harmony may shift position i.e., it may move between a root position and an inversion or visa versa, or (ii) the harmony may change altogether as the resolution arrives.

Let's take a straightforward suspension example and then rewrite it to reflect the possible changes as outlined above.

In this case the harmony shifts position from chord **I** to **Ib** as the suspension resolves.

Here, the harmony changes from chord **I** to **vi** as the suspension resolves.

Audio 1.18

As the suspension resolves listen to (i) the change of position and (ii) the change of chord.

Exercise 1.15

The following short extracts from Bach Chorales demonstrate suspensions with various resolutions. Firstly, add roman numerals to analyse the progressions where the line extends (in some extracts not all chords are required). Secondly, draw a box around each suspension together with its resolution. Finally, tick the sentence appropriate to each resolution. Where there are 2 suspensions, tick to the left of the sentence for the first and to the right for the second.

Resolves normally
Resolves ornamentally
Resolves as the chord shifts position
Resolves as the harmony changes

Numerals ______________________________

Resolves normally
Resolves ornamentally
Resolves as the chord shifts position
Resolves as the harmony changes

Numerals ______________________________

Resolves normally
Resolves ornamentally
Resolves as the chord shifts position
Resolves as the harmony changes

Numerals ____________________

Resolves normally
Resolves ornamentally
Resolves as the chord shifts position
Resolves as the harmony changes

Numerals ______________

Resolves normally
Resolves ornamentally
Resolves as the chord shifts position
Resolves as the harmony changes

Numerals ______________________________

Resolves normally
Resolves ornamentally
Resolves as the chord shifts position
Resolves as the harmony changes

Numerals ____________

Resolves normally
Resolves ornamentally
Resolves as the chord shifts position
Resolves as the harmony changes

Numerals ______________________________

Resolves normally
Resolves ornamentally
Resolves as the chord shifts position
Resolves as the harmony changes

Numerals ____________

Resolves normally
Resolves ornamentally
Resolves as the chord shifts position
Resolves as the harmony changes

Numerals ______________________________

CHAPTER 2

ACCENTED PASSING NOTES

To appreciate the effect of accented passing notes, listen to the two examples printed below. First you hear a harmonisation with unaccented passing notes followed by the same harmonisation using **accented** passing notes. All passing notes are circled.

Audio 2.1

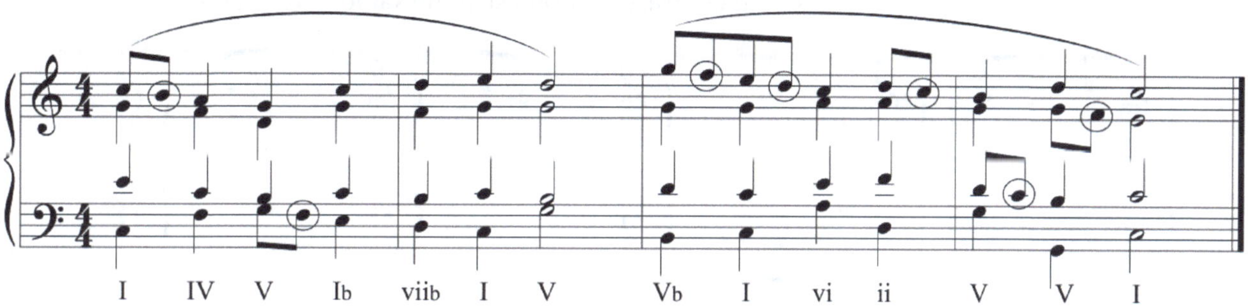

A few points to note . . .

- The pitch of the passing note does not change, however, its rhythmic placement does.
- The passing note is now placed on the accented part of the beat, thus creating a dissonance with the chord notes.
- The overall effect of the dissonant accented note is to give the music a sense of forward movement.

Because the accented passing note forms a dissonance, its use is somewhat more restricted than an unaccented passing note. It may be useful to consider accented passing notes in two situations (i) where there is no chord change, and (ii) where there is a chord change.

No chord change

Where there is no chord change accented passing notes are reasonably free in their use.

They may be used . . .

- Descending or ascending.
- Singly in any voice part.
- In pairs moving in parallel 3^{rds} or 6^{ths}.
- In contrary motion using the same letter name.

Audio 2.2

Listen to the above snippets demonstrating the various possibilities.

A point to be mindful of . . .

Don't **strike** the accented passing note with the pitch that it is resolving to.

C in the tenor part is **struck** with the accented passing note in the soprano – best avoided!

However, in this instance, although C is present in the tenor it is **sustained** from the previous beat rather than being struck. This is acceptable.

In this instance, the C in the bass part is struck with the accented passing note in the soprano. This is acceptable because it is in the bass part (as with a suspension).

With a chord change

Where there is a chord change it is best practice to . . .

- Use accented passing notes **descending** in any upper voice.
- In the bass voice use a descending accented passing note always resolving to a first inversion chord (as with a suspension).

Here the accented passing note descends as the harmony changes. It also occupies a full accented crotchet beat.

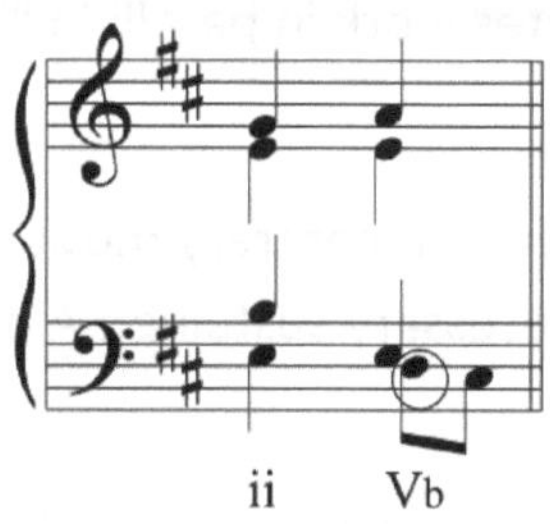

The accented passing note in the bass descends, moving to a first inversion chord. Note the necessary doubling of the 5th.

In relation to the above, be mindful of the doubling which is used in order to avoid a mistake of parallel 5ths.

Audio 2.3

Listen to the following worked example in A minor. Pay special attention to the circled accented passing notes while studying the points below.

Bar 1, beat 2: Notice the A in the tenor part is sustained rather than struck, allowing the correct use of the accented passing note in the soprano.

Bar 2, beat 3: Here the accented passing notes work in parallel 6[ths] in the soprano and tenor voices.

Bar 3, beat 2: The accented passing notes work in contrary motion in soprano and bass voices. Also note the necessary sustained A in the tenor part.

Bar 4, beat 3: The accented passing note is possible in the alto voice while the E is **sustained** in the soprano part.

Bar 5, beats 1 and 3: The soprano has two examples of effective accented passing notes as the harmonies change.

Exercise 2.1

Add roman numerals to each of the following. Rewrite to include accented passing notes where appropriate.

(a)

Numerals ____

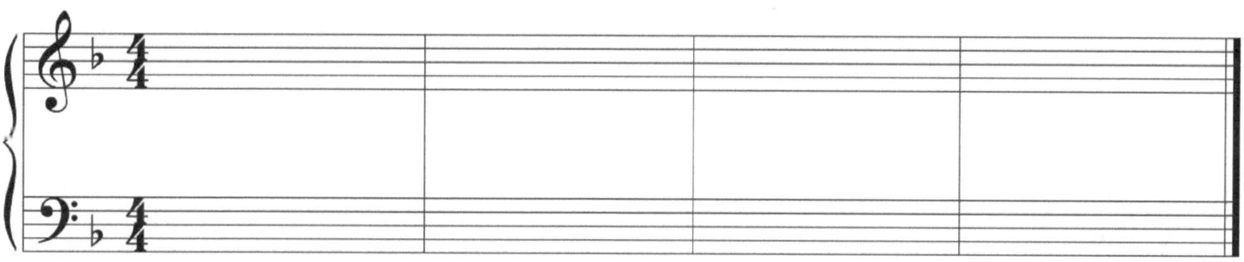

(b)

Numerals ____

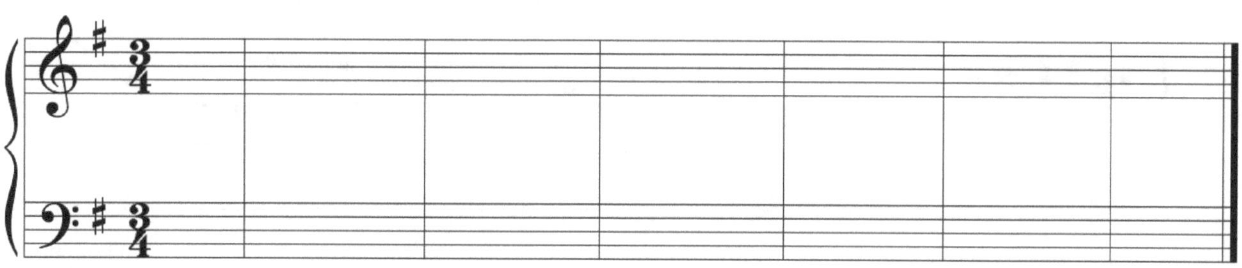

Exercise 2.2

Indicate your choice of harmony by adding roman numerals to each bass line. Remember the possibility of accented passing notes being present in the bass. Then write a complete soprano line making some use of accented passing notes.

(a)

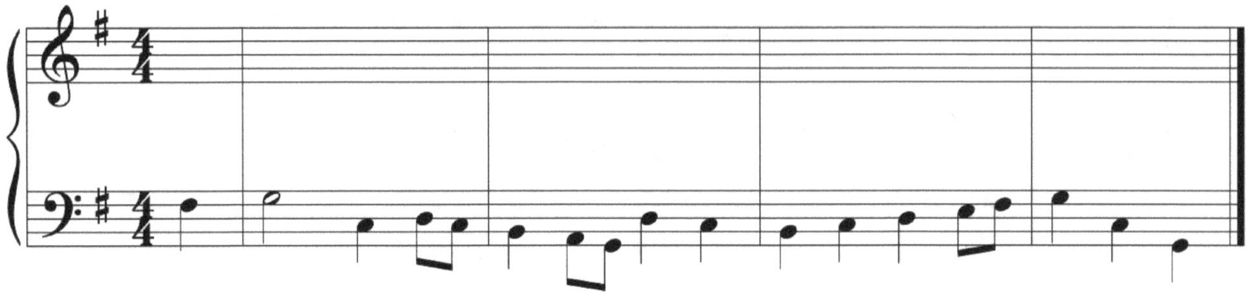

Numerals ______________________________

(b)

Numerals ______________________________

(c)

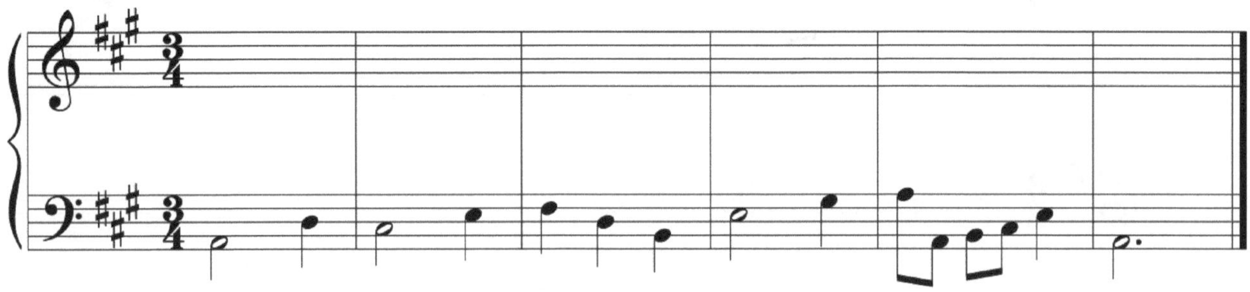

Numerals ______________________________

Harmonising a soprano melody

In a melodic profile containing a lot of stepwise motion, how is the distinction made between unaccented and accented passing notes? Here is a suggested method of working. Let us examine the melodic fragment below.

Technically it would seem possible to treat it in two ways:

Firstly, with **unaccented** passing and auxiliary notes (these are circled). Begin by singing the decorated version, then strip out the unaccented quavers and sing again to reveal a basic framework.

Secondly, with **accented** passing notes (these are circled). Once again sing the decorated version. Then strip out the accented quavers to reveal a different framework.

Sing and compare each of the melodic frameworks.

Which do you consider gives the more musical and natural shaping?

This approach is the best guideline in helping you decide what should be harmonised.

On balance, the second example is the more attractive of the two.

The next step is to choose chords for the basic framework.

Finally, reinsert the decorative notes and add alto and tenor parts to complete the harmonisation.

Audio 2.4

Listen to both examples above to hear the step-by-step process.

Let us study another worked example while following the step-by-step approach.

Take phrase 1 to begin; technically it can be treated in two ways as follows: (i) by circling accented passing notes and (ii) by circling unaccented passing notes to reveal two different frameworks.

Sing both to decide which shape is more musically appealing – on balance the first framework is more natural.

Here is a possible harmonisation.

Let us now consider the second phrase marking both accented and unaccented passing notes as before.

Sing both fragments for comparison. Each has attractive elements. However, in this instance a mix of the two creates the best solution.

Next, a possible bass line with chosen chords is added.

Finally, the harmonisation is completed by adding alto and tenor parts. All non-harmony notes in the melody are circled.

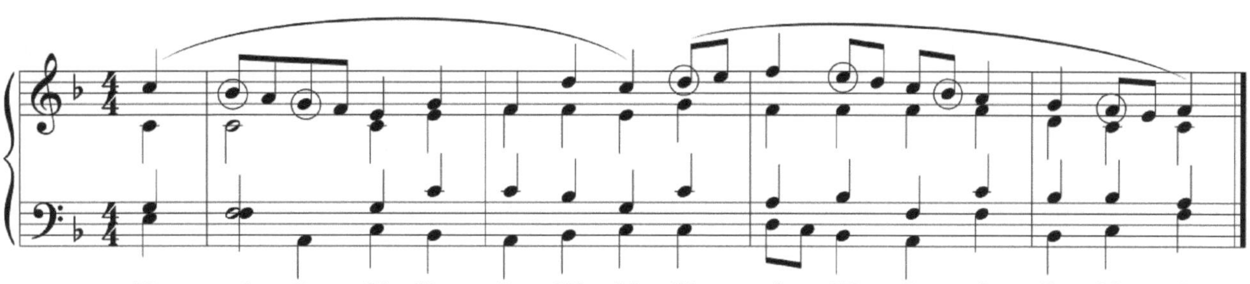

Accented passing notes, like suspensions, create dissonant decoration, therefore the accented dissonant pitch with its resolution is shown in the figured bass. The full harmonisation is shown again here to include the figured bass.

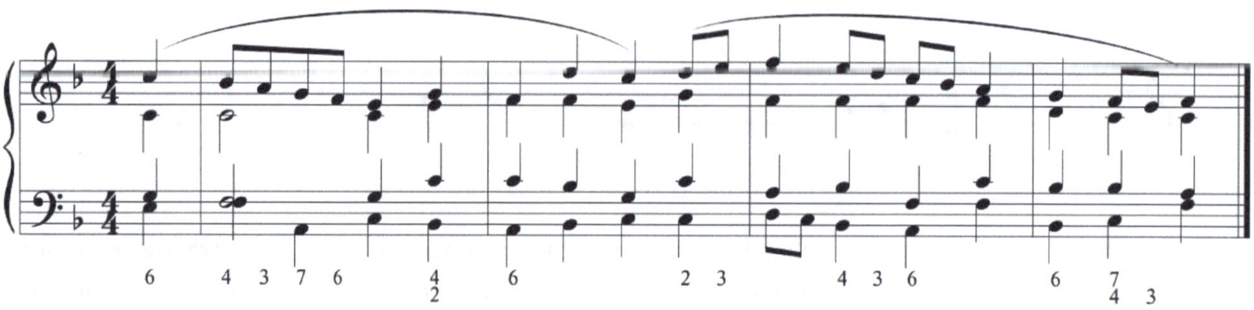

Audio 2.5

Listen carefully to the completed harmonisation. Notice the effect of the accented passing notes in creating natural tension and release, thus giving the music forward momentum.

Exercise 2.3

The following melodies contain a mixture of unaccented and accented passing notes. Sing each melody in the manner that has been outlined in previous examples to help determine the best underlying framework. Then harmonise for SATB.

(a)

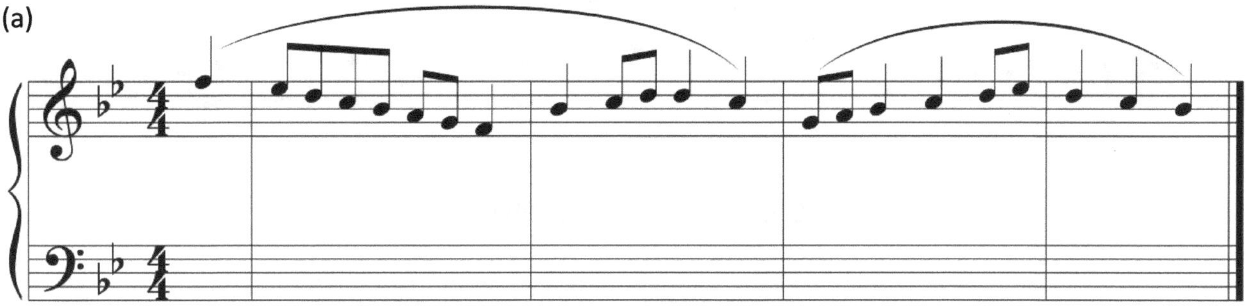

Numerals ____________________

(b)

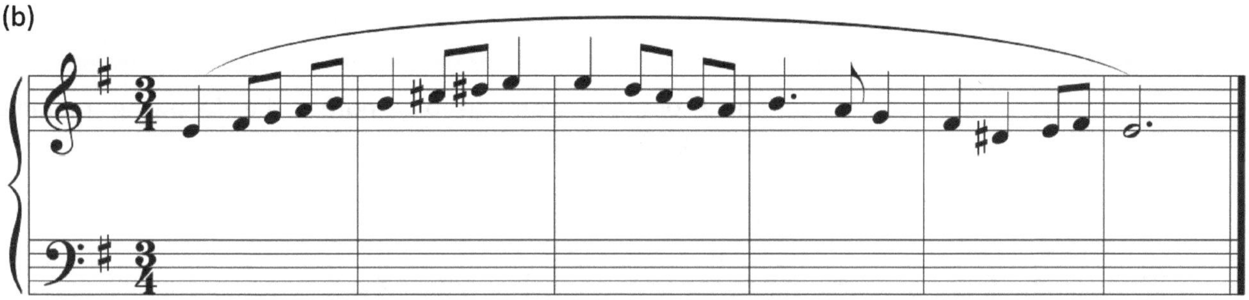

Numerals ____________________

(c)

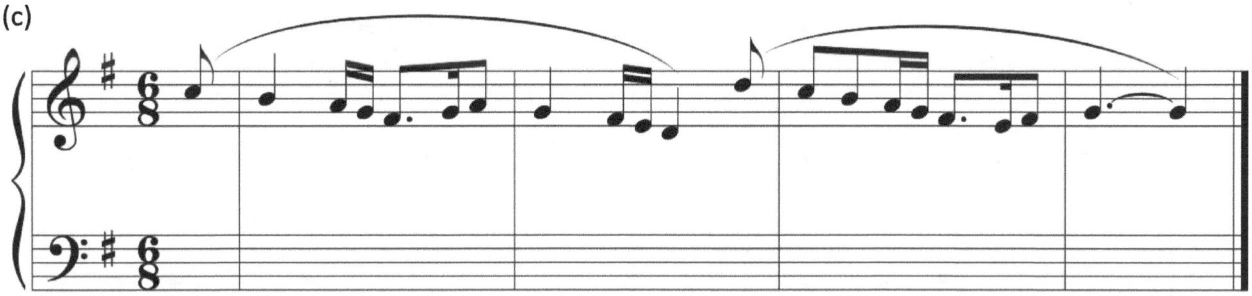

Numerals ____________________

(d)

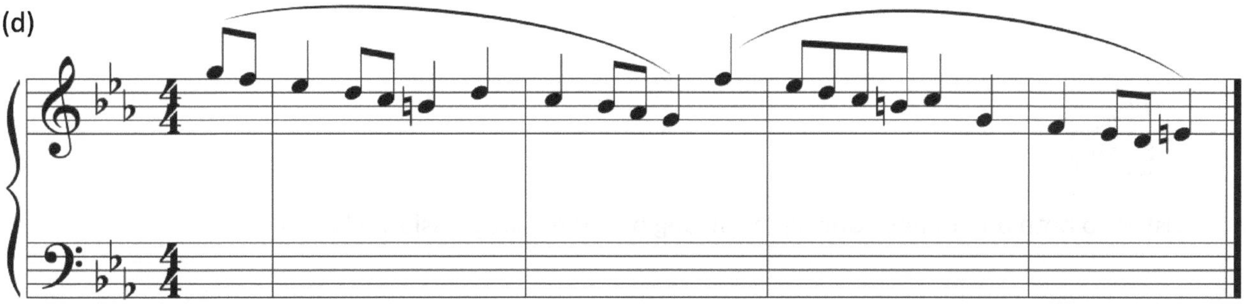

Numerals ____________________

The following worked example draws together all decorative elements studied to date. Sing the melody as often as needed in order to recognise the decoration and reveal the most musical framework.

Below is a musical possibility.

Stripping out the non-harmony notes, the following melodic framework retains the fundamental profile of the line.

An effective harmonisation is outlined below.

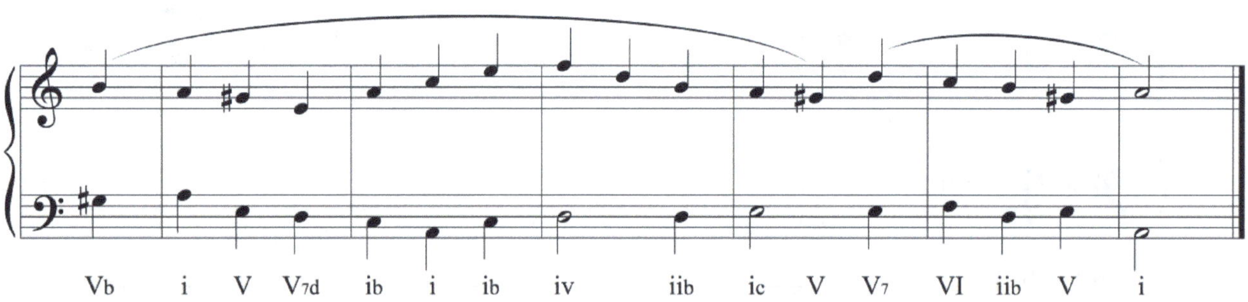

Audio 2.6

Listen to both outer lines noticing the strong harmonic progressions chosen.

Below is a complete 4-part harmonisation which reinserts the original decoration before adding inner voices to ensure correct detail in the part writing.

Audio 2.7

Listen to the above example paying particular attention to the enhanced effect created by the decoration.

A final consideration is to look at the possibility of including additional decoration to the added parts. All dissonant decoration is reflected in the figured bass.

Audio 2.8

Listen once more to appreciate the extra detail. Of particular interest is the addition of the 7th on the last quaver in bar 5 to facilitate a double suspension in the final bar.

Exercise 2.4

Harmonise each of the following soprano melodies for SATB. Begin by singing the melody to determine the harmonic framework. Complete the bass line before adding alto and tenor parts.

(a)

Numerals ______________________________

(b)

Numerals ______________________________

Exercise 2.5

Add roman numerals, then complete the harmonisation by adding parts for alto and tenor voices in accordance with the figured bass.

(a)

Numerals ______________________________

(b)

Numerals ____________________

CHAPTER 3

MELODIC MINOR HARMONISATION

Our harmony so far has relied on chords formed from the harmonic minor scale. A limitation can arise if the 6th and 7th notes follow one another as chord notes in a melodic line, giving rise to the interval of an augmented 2nd (***f – si***). Augmented intervals are **always** avoided in any of the melodic lines.

In certain contexts, it is possible to use the melodic minor form to build chords as outlined below.

Let us look at the ascending scale involving the raised 6th (***fi***).

Be aware that the quality of the chords will change when using the raised 6th as seen below.

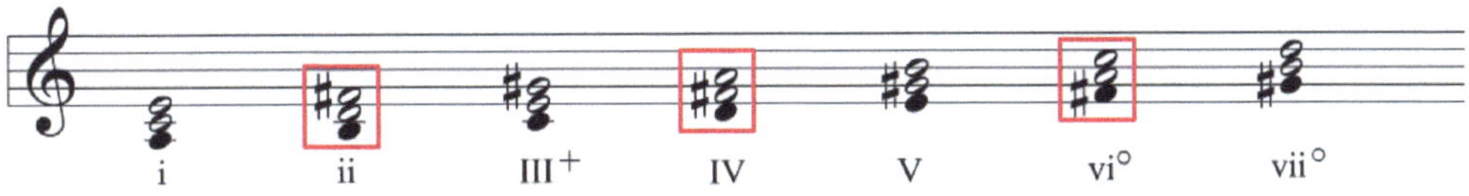

- chord **ii** changes to minor
- chord **IV** changes to major
- chord **vi°** changes to diminished

Possible harmonisation using the ascending form

This harmonisation tends to be idiomatic; it is generally presented in either of these forms:

Possible harmonisations with ***m fi si l*** in the soprano are as follows:

Notice in **IV – V** that the soprano rises in 3[rds] with the bass. However, it is essential that the other voices move in contrary motion to the bass in order to avoid parallel 5[ths] and 8[vs].

As chord **i** moves to **iib** it is necessary to double the 5th in chord **i** to avoid consecutive 5[ths] with the soprano line.

This is a strong harmonisation with no difficulty in the part writing.

Audio 3.1

Listen to the three examples above.

Possible harmonisations with *l fi si l* in the soprano are as follows:

Audio 3.2

Listen to the above harmonisations.

The part writing in the previous progressions presents no difficulty. However, always avoid doubling the raised 6th.

The melodic minor idiom also forms a strong bass line shape with harmonisation as follows:

You may remember the necessary triadic layout required for stepwise first inversion chords and the obligatory alternate doubling which is applied here.

Remember the raised 6th is **not** an option for doubling

Audio 3.3

Listen to the above examples paying particular attention to the melodic minor bass line.

Study the following worked example.

In this fragment the melodic minor idioms are highlighted as they appear in the soprano and bass lines.

Audio 3.4

Listen to the given sections of soprano and bass lines.

The next step is to complete the missing bars of the soprano and bass lines. Roman numerals indicate the chosen harmony.

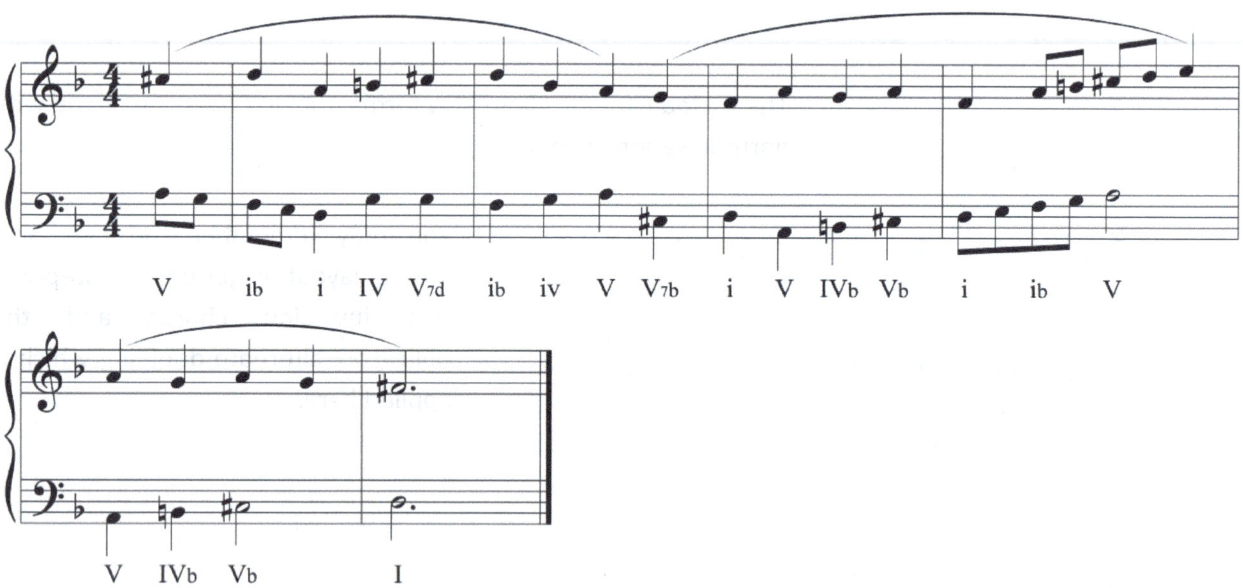

Audio 3.5

Now listen to the completed soprano and bass lines.

Finally, the harmonisation is completed by adding parts for alto and tenor voices. Study the part writing in detail.

Audio 3.6

Listen to the 4-part harmonisation. Notice the ascending melodic minor shaping in the soprano of bar 4. B natural is best treated as a passing note because of the quaver rhythm.

Although the harmonisation is correct it lacks flow and interest in some areas. The final step is to draw in the various types of decoration studied so far to enhance the overall musicality.

Figured bass highlights the added dissonant decoration. Some inner detail is changed in bar 3 to allow for the added suspension.

Audio 3.7

Listen as you study the final version appreciating the steps taken in order to create an interesting and musical outcome.

Exercise 3.1

Harmonise the following melodic minor idioms for SATB.

(a)

Numerals ____________________

(b)

Numerals ____________________

Now consider the descending melodic minor scale involving the lowered 7th (sometimes referred to as the flattened 7th).

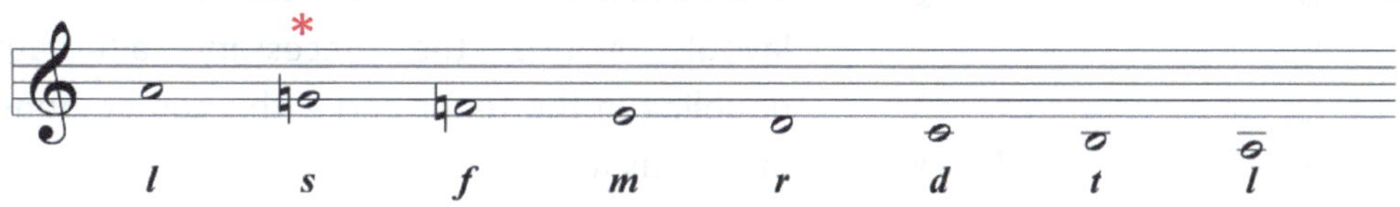

Again, notice that the quality of the chords will change when using the lowered 7th as outlined below.

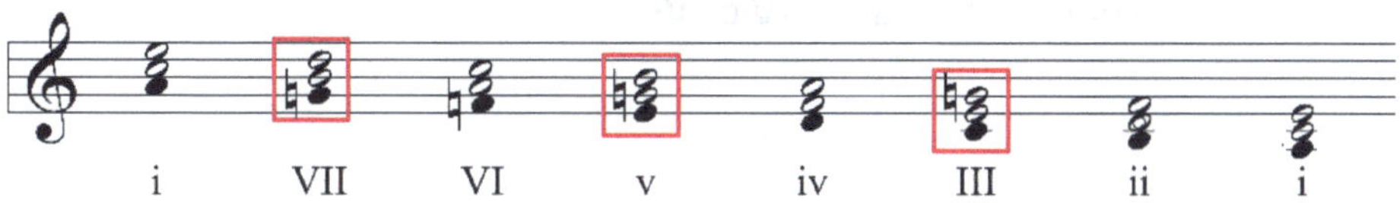

- Chord **VII** changes to major.
- Chord **v** changes to minor.
- Chord **III** changes to major

Possible harmonisation using the descending form

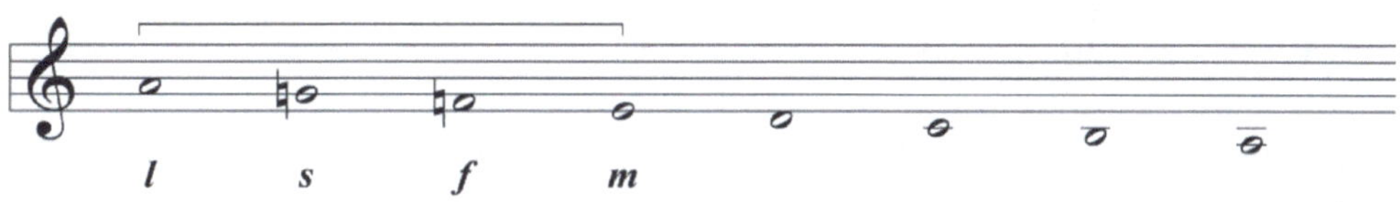

The descending idiom is generally presented in this form:

Possible harmonisations with ***l s f m*** in the soprano are shown below.

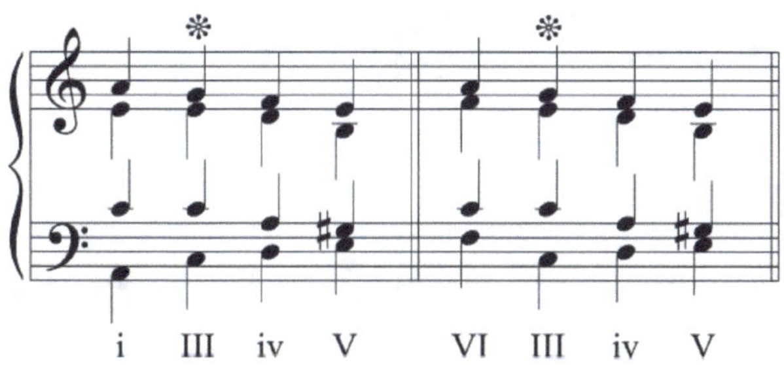

Chords **III – iv – V**; 3 root position chords rising by step in the bass part – use the typical descending movement in all the upper parts.

Chords **ib – VIIb – VIb – Vb**; 4 first inversion chords falling by step – use the typical triadic layout. Notice the necessary alternate doubling in the tenor part – this can be done in various ways.

- Remember to restore the raised 7th accidental in the final chord of the idiom (**V** or **Vb**).

Audio 3.8

Listen to the four previous harmonised idioms as you study the examples.

The descending idiom also forms a strong bass line with harmonisations as follows.

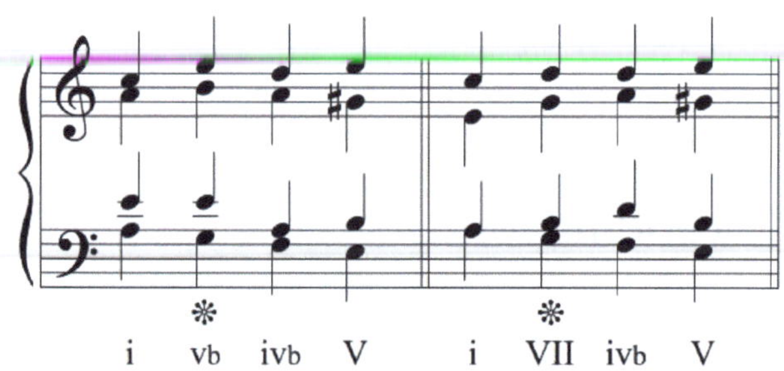

Audio 3.9

Listen to the progressions with the idiom in the bass part.

Exercise 3.2

Harmonise the following melodic minor idioms for SATB.

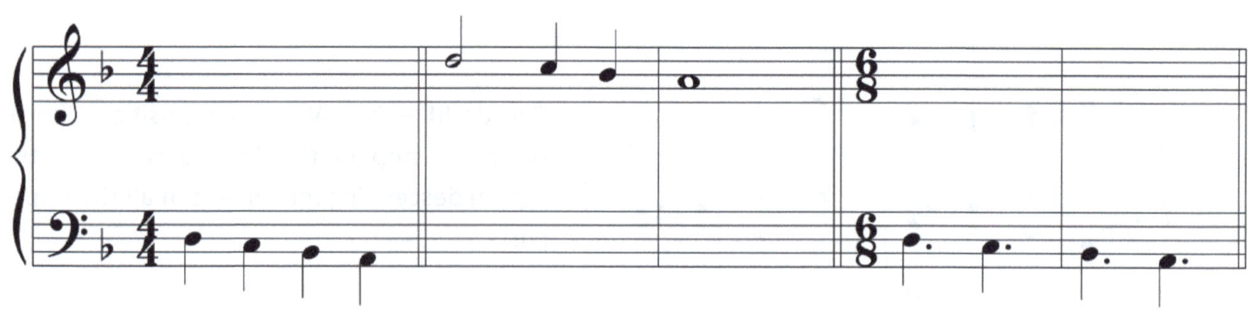

Numerals ____

Here is a worked example combining both melodic minor profiles. The melodic minor idioms are highlighted, and the opening harmony is included.

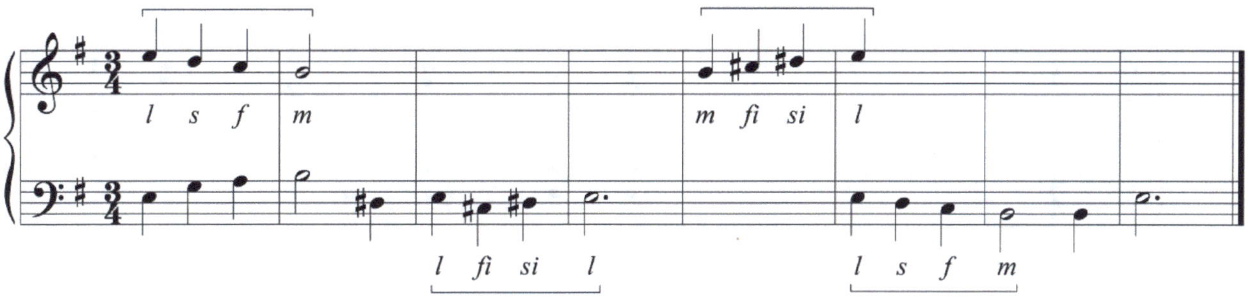

Audio 3.10

Listen to the fragments of the given lines.

The next stage is to complete the missing sections of the soprano and bass lines. Roman numerals indicate the chosen harmony.

Audio 3.11

You now hear the completed soprano and bass lines.

Finally, the harmonisation is completed by adding parts for alto and tenor. Study the part writing carefully.

Audio 3.12

Listen to the basic 4-part harmonisation.

This basic harmonisation, while correct, needs some decoration for interest. Figured bass highlights the added dissonant decoration.

Audio 3.13

Listen as you study the final version, noting the musical interest created by the added decoration.

Exercise 3.3

Complete the following exercises in two stages: -

(i) Add roman numerals according to the figured bass and complete the harmonisation by adding alto and tenor parts.

(ii) Consider your harmonisation once more with a view to adding some appropriate decoration. Suggestions are indicated by way of the revised figured bass, but other possibilities may also be incorporated.

A (i)

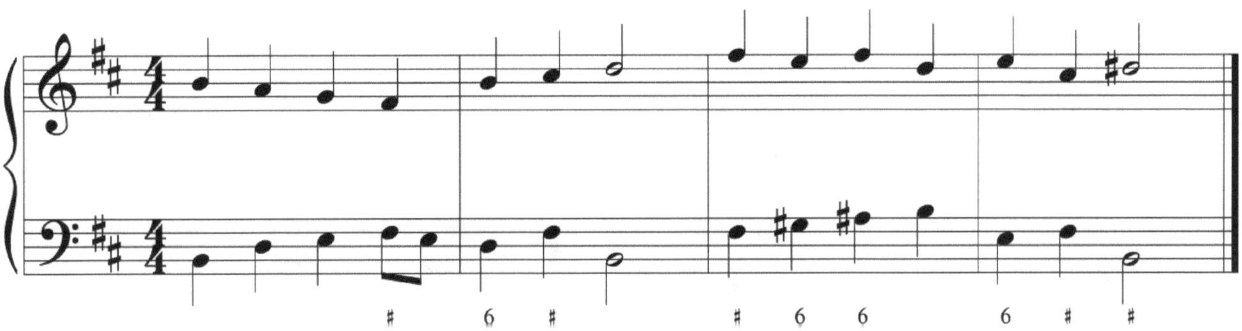

Numerals ____

A (ii)

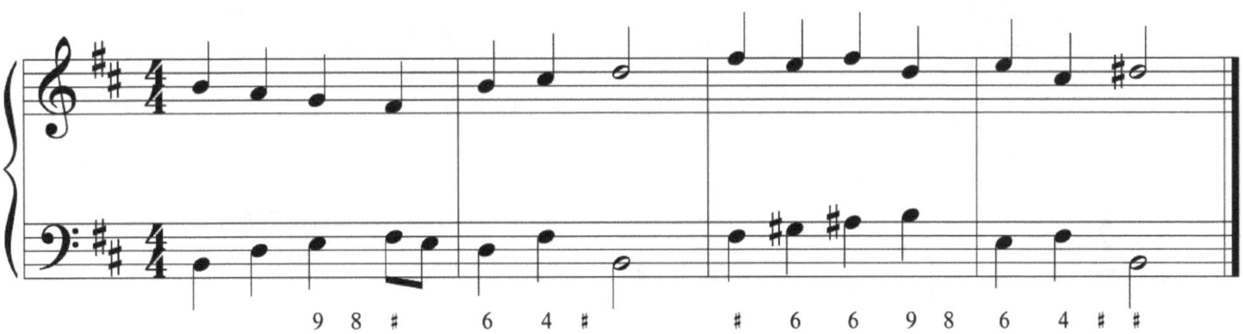

B (i)

Numerals

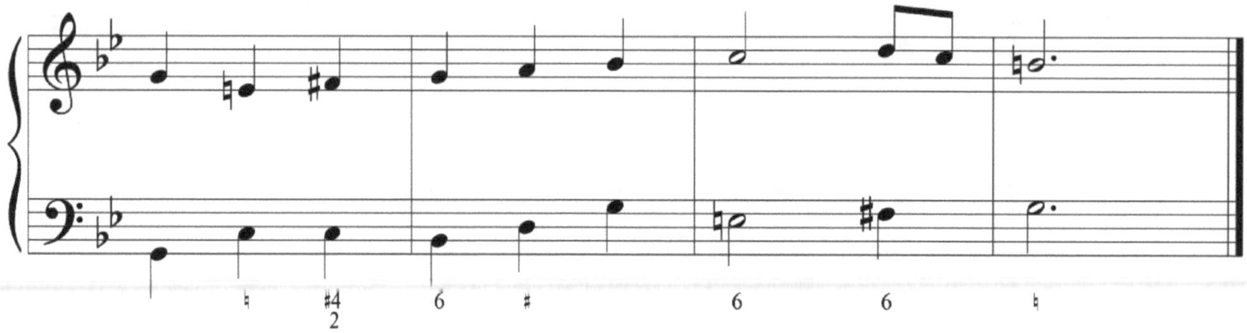

B (ii)

C (i)

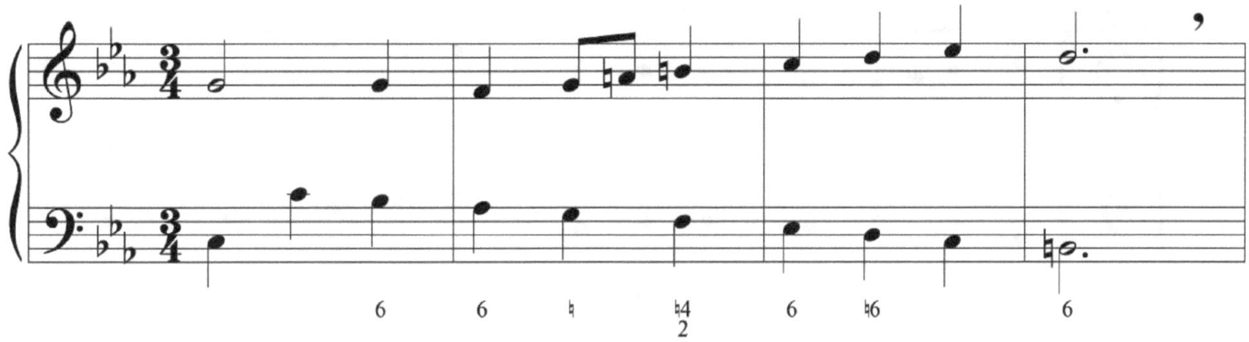

Numerals ____________________

____

C (ii)

D (i)

Numerals ______________________________

____

D (ii)

CHAPTER 4

HARMONIC ANALYSIS 1

So far, the emphasis has been on vocal settings. However, in the following analysis pieces you will encounter the harmonic knowledge that you have acquired thus far in the context of simple keyboard extracts as well as vocal. The analysis is linked to aural/visual observation where you will hear the music while following the printed score. While some extracts are from the beginning of a piece or movement, others are not. For the sake of simplicity in bar numbering all extracts will be taken as beginning with bar 1.

The extracts in this chapter are taken from Baroque and Classical literature. You may listen to each as often as you wish.

Exercise 4.1 Audio 4.1

Listen as you study this extract from Bach's Goldberg Variations BWV 988 Var.18. Then answer the questions that follow.

(i) In this short extract there are four instances of tied notes but only one is a suspension – mark it with X.

(ii) Circle two examples of accented auxiliary notes.

(iii) Analyse the harmonies by writing the roman numerals below the bass stave.

Exercise 4.2 Audio 4.2a/b/c

Below is a group of Bach chorale phrases. Answer the questions in relation to each.

(a)

(i) Circle an accented passing note in bar 1

(ii) Draw a box around a suspension and its resolution in bar 2.

(b)

(i) What is the function of the boxed notes in the tenor line? ____________________.

(ii) Is the circled note in the soprano line a passing note or an auxiliary note? ____________.

(c)

(i) Name the key of the phrase. _______. Explain the C sharp in the final chord __________.

(ii) What is the function of the circled notes in the soprano line? ________________.

Exercise 4.3 Audio 4.3

Listen to and study the extract below from a movement of Haydn's piano sonata in C Hob 16. Then answer the questions that follow.

(i) Analyse the harmonies in bars 4 and 5 by writing the roman numerals below the bass stave.

(ii) Circle any two examples of accented passing notes.

(iii) Identify and circle an example of a double suspension and add the figured bass at the appropriate point below the stave.

Exercise 4.4 Audio 4.4a/b/c

Below is a group of Bach chorale phrases. Answer the questions in relation to each.

(a)

Liebster Jesu, wir sind hier

(i) Explain the function of the tied note in the bass of bar 1. _________________.

(ii) Circle two examples of accented passing notes in the phrase.

(iii) How many times does the dominant chord feature? ________.

(b)

Christum wir sollen loben sehon

(i) Name the key of the phrase. _________. Add roman numerals below the bass in bar 1.

(ii) Explain the presence of C sharp in the bass in bar 1 on beat 3. _________________.

(iii) What is the function of the circled note in the alto part in bar 2? _________.

(c)

Durch Adams Fall

(i) The phrase is in the key of C minor; identify the melodic minor harmonisation by drawing a bracket below where it occurs.

(ii) Circle two examples of suspension decoration and add the figured bass at the appropriate points.

Exercise 4.5 Audio 4.5

This short extract is from Sonata in C minor K457 by Mozart. Circle all suspensions.

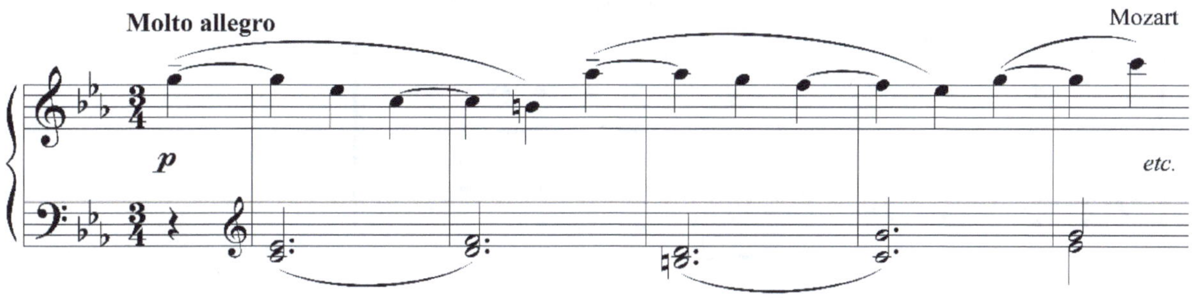

Exercise 4.6 Audio 4.6

This extract is from Beethoven's Sonata in D minor Op.31, No.2. Answer the questions that follow.

(i) Analyse the harmonies by writing the roman numerals below the stave in bars 1 – 3.

(ii) Circle all examples of suspensions in the quaver area marked by a bracket in bars 2 and 3.

(iii) The boxed area in line 2 forms a sequence with the preceding quaver movement but is now transposed to G minor. Circle the suspensions in the treble.

Exercise 4.7 Audio 4.7a/b/c

Listen to and study this final group of chorale phrases, then answer the questions that follow.

Nun freut euch, Gottes Kinder all

(i) Taking account of the accidentals, name the key of the phrase ____________.

(ii) Comment on the final chord. __________________.

(iii) Add roman numerals below the first four chords.

(iv) Locate and circle an example of a suspension.

Wer Gott vertraut

(i) Which voice part has a chain of suspension decoration? __________.

(ii) Circle each suspension.

(iii) Add roman numerals below the first four chords.

O wie selig seid ihr doch

(i) Circle an example of each: an accented passing note and double accented passing notes.

(ii) Draw a bracket/s where melodic minor harmonisation is a feature.

(iii) Add figured bass below the first phrase.

CHAPTER 5

MODULATION Part 1
Dominant and relative (major keys)

Modulation is the process of changing from one key to another. Composers use this to provide new tonal interest. Elementary modulation normally moves within the range of 5 closely related keys. From the original tonic these are:

- relative of the tonic
- dominant (moving to the sharp side of the key)
- subdominant (moving to the flat side of the key)
- relative of the dominant
- relative of the subdominant

The following diagram shows the relationship of each to the tonic.

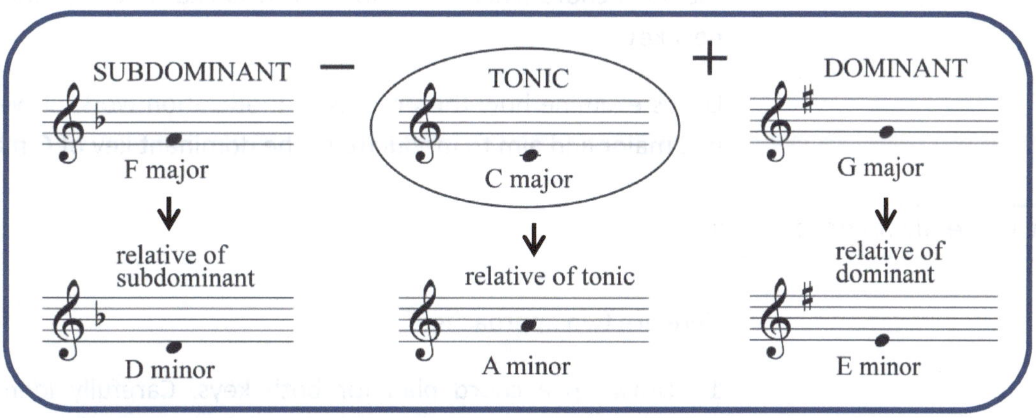

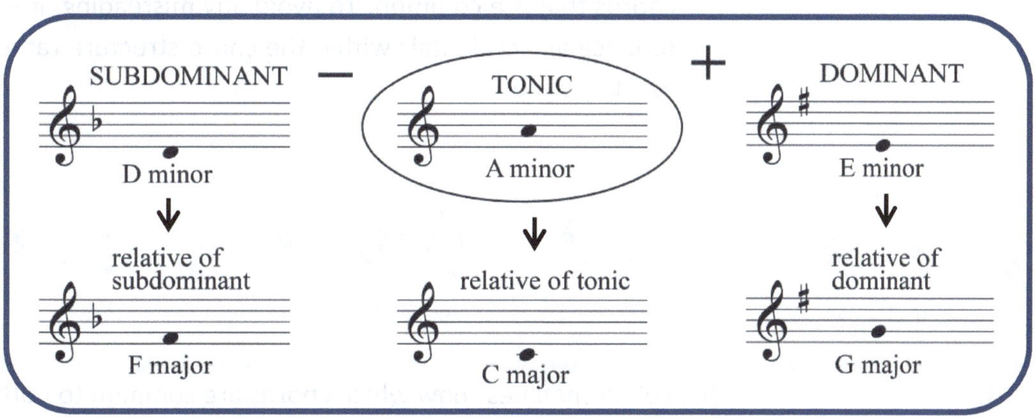

Modulation from a major key to its dominant

Modulation from a major key to its nearest neighbour, the dominant, is the modulation most commonly heard.

Audio 5.1

Listen to this short extract from Schumann's piano piece *'Merry Peasant'* from his Album for the Young Op. 68. The music moves from F major to the dominant key of C major in the last bar. Notice how the new tonal centre creates a 'brighter' sound.

Pivot

The smoothest way to move from one key to another is by means of a **pivot** chord. The pivot chord must have **all** its notes common to both keys. This chord is used as a turning point creating a smooth pathway into the new key. It is common practice to label the pivot chord twice, firstly in the original key and secondly in the new key.

Let us examine how the process of modulation works if we begin in C major and aim to modulate to the dominant key of G major.

How is the pivot chord selected?

Here are two approaches:

1. Draw up a chord plan for both keys. Carefully identify all chords that are common. To avoid any misreading, it is useful to place all accidentals within the chord structure rather than as a key signature.

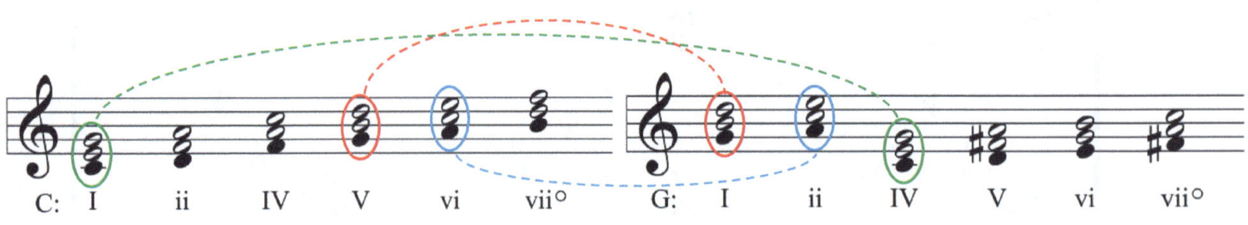

The colour matches show which chords are common to both keys.

2. Identify what is **different** between the two keys and make sure to avoid this note being present in any common chord. In this specific case the pivot chord must **not** contain an '**F**'.

Where is the pivot chord placed?

Normally the tonic key is established before any modulation is made. The tonic key could be determined by a complete phrase or a portion of a phrase. The inclusion of both the tonic and dominant chords will clarify the home key. As the harmony progresses, a common chord may occur at any point. Once chosen, the chord is labelled twice; first in the tonic key and then in the new key as follows:

C	I	C	V	C	vi
G	IV	G	I	G	ii

Thereafter, the harmony as it progresses in the new key, will be labelled in the new key.

Be mindful of any accidentals which belong to the new key and remember to include them as they are vital to the new tonality.

How is the new key established?

Once the pivot chord has been identified the music normally progresses to a cadence point in the new key. This is often a perfect cadence.

Here is an example demonstrating a modulation from C major to G major.

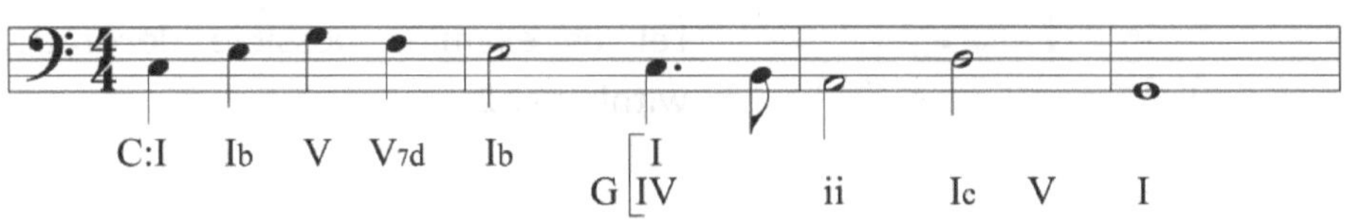

In close key relationships such as tonic and dominant, where many pivot chords are available, there may be several points at which the shift to the new key may be marked.

Here the pivot chord is marked earlier.

Alternatively, another possibility is to mark the pivot chord later.

Note that root position and 1st inversion chords may act as a pivot. However, avoid selecting **any 2nd inversion** chord as a pivot since it functions only as a decoration.

> Although the pivot chord may be marked in different locations, the **sound** of the new key does not emerge until its accidental is heard.

Now we complete the harmonisation adding the soprano line first followed by the alto and tenor parts.

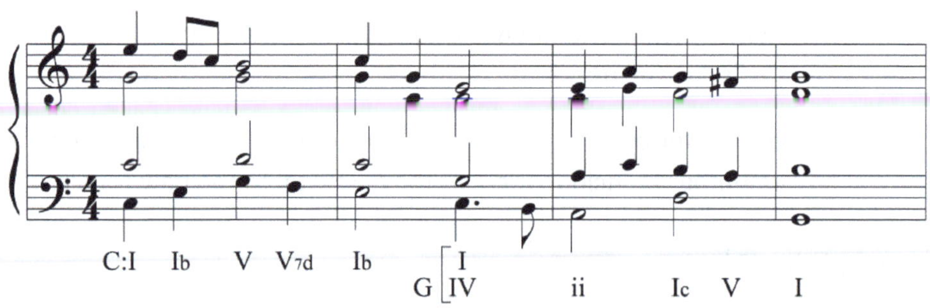

Audio 5.2

Listen to the harmonised fragment noting the change to G major at the end of the phrase.

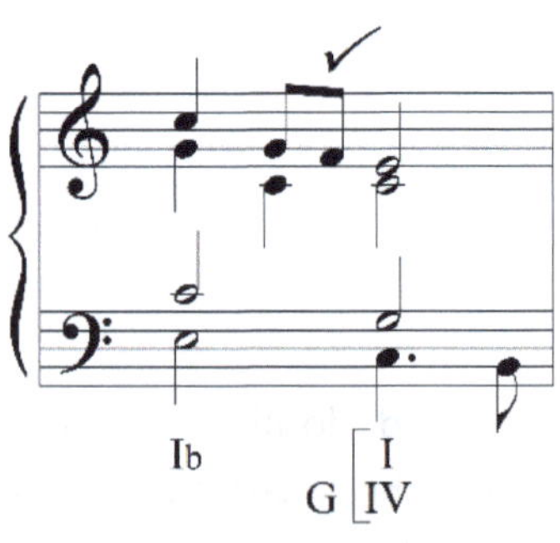

Let us examine possible decoration within bar 2.

Once the pivot chord is marked, the thinking should be in terms of the new key. However, the new accidental F sharp is best introduced first as a **harmony note** rather than as decoration.

> Introduce the new accidental as a **chord** note

In the initial stages of understanding modulation, we will focus only on the outward journey from the tonic to the new key. In later chapters a return to the home key will be included and further keys will be explored.

Exercise 5.1

In these exercises the location of the pivot chord has been marked. Each new key is established with a perfect cadence. Add roman numerals. Then add alto and tenor parts. Take care to include the new accidental.

(a)

Numerals ____

(b)

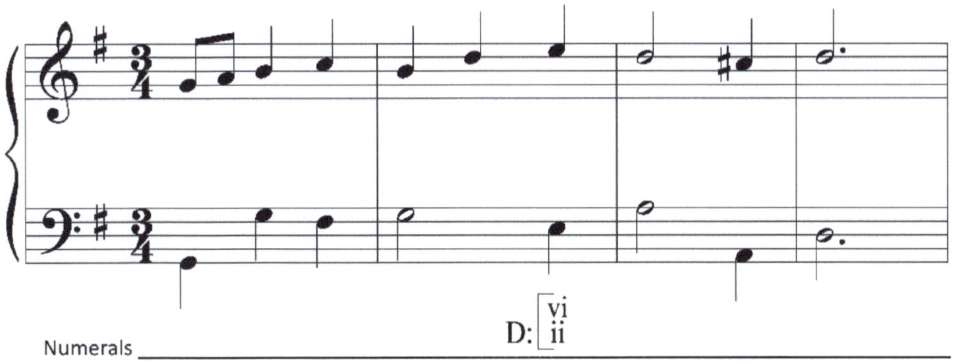

Numerals ____

Exercise 5.2

Label the given bass carefully deciding a suitable location for the pivot chord. The new key is established with a perfect cadence. Complete the soprano first followed by the alto and tenor parts. Remember to include the new accidental.

(a)

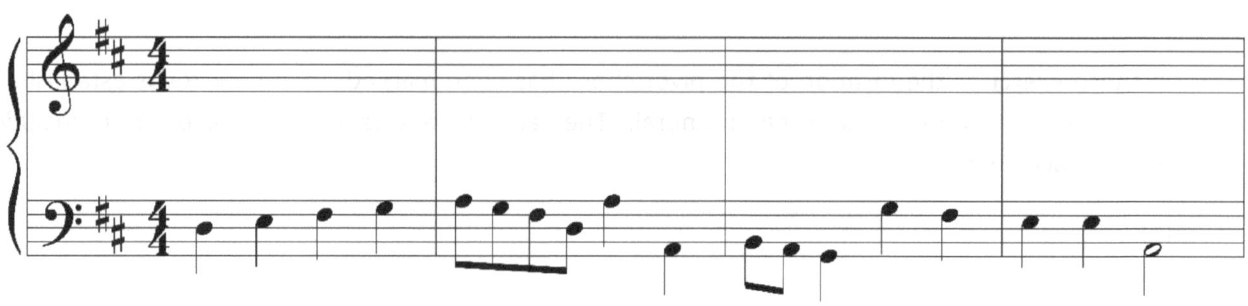

Numerals ____

(b)

Numerals ____

Modulation from a major key to its relative minor

Audio 5.3

To hear the effect of modulating from a major key to its relative minor, listen to this short extract from Schumann's piano piece *'A little Hunting Song'* from his Album for the Young Op. 68. The music moves from F major to D minor in bars 5 - 8.

Let us take an example to demonstrate a modulation from C major to A minor. The first step is to select all **common** chords between these keys.

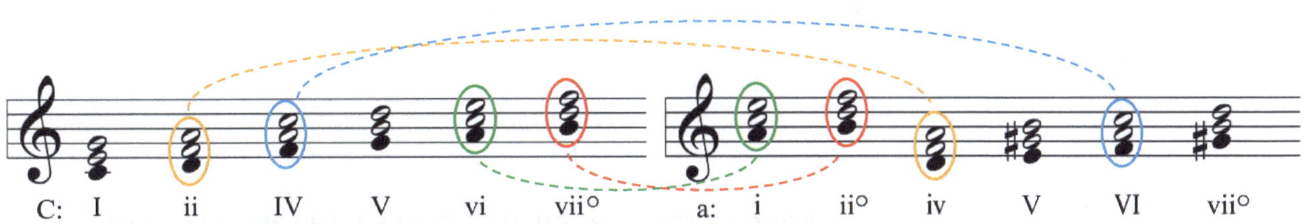

The colour matches clearly show that there are 4 pivot chord options available.

Another way to approach this is to identify what is **different** between the 2 keys, namely G/G sharp. The pivot chord must **not** contain this pitch.

We begin with a bass line showing a pivot chord in bar 2.

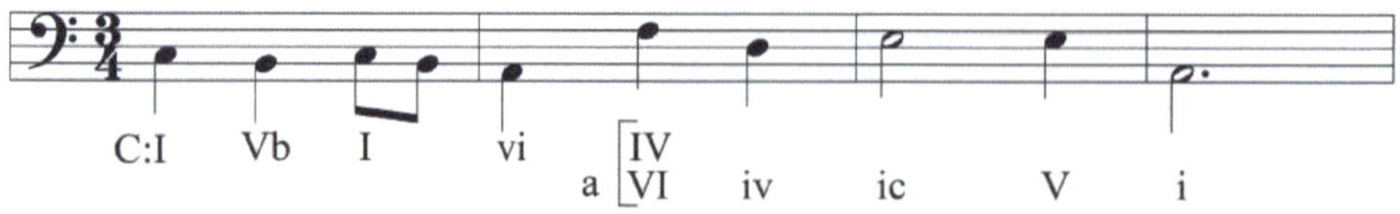

Alternatively, the pivot chord may be marked a beat earlier.

The pivot chord may also be marked a beat later.

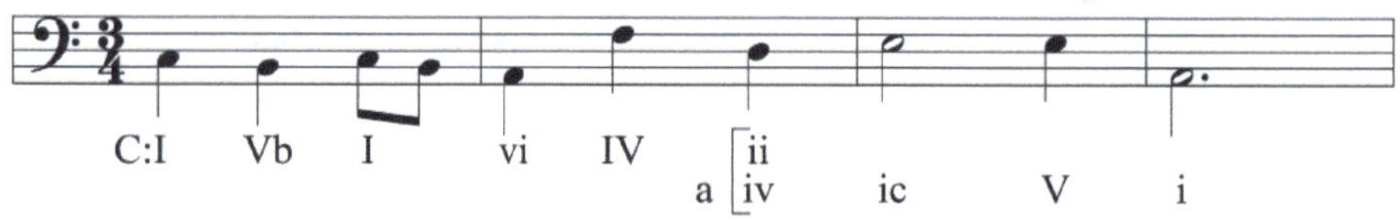

Once the pivot chord is marked, think ahead in the new key. Remember the new G sharp accidental is best heard initially as a harmony note.

Now we complete the harmonisation adding the soprano line first followed by alto and tenor parts.

Take note that the sound of the new key will only emerge when the accidental G sharp is heard in bar 3 tenor part.

Audio 5.4

Listen to the phrase beginning in C major and modulating to A minor. A minor is established with a perfect cadence at the end of the phrase.

Exercise 5.3

In these exercises the location of the pivot chord has been marked *. Each new key is established with a perfect cadence. Add roman numerals, then add alto and tenor parts. Take care to include the new accidental.

(a)

Numerals ____

(b)

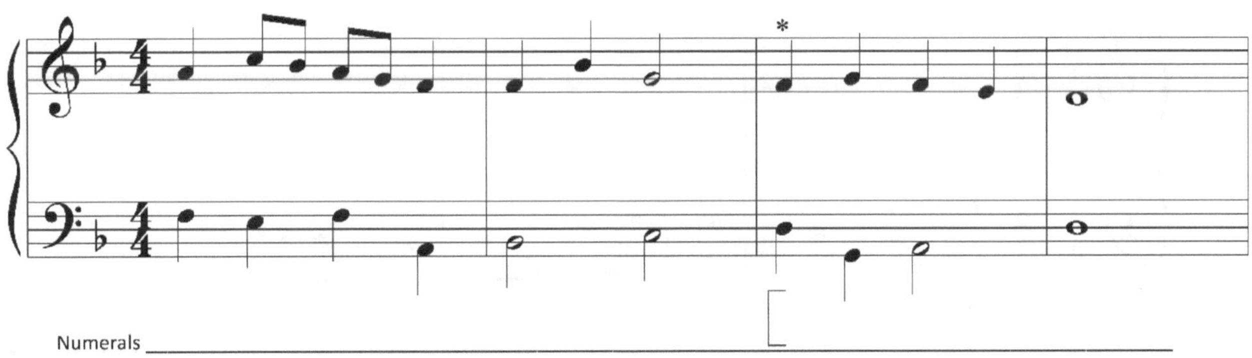

Numerals ____

Exercise 5.4

Label the bass carefully deciding a suitable location for the pivot chord. The new key is established with a perfect cadence. Complete the soprano line first followed by the alto and tenor parts. Remember to include the new accidental.

(a)

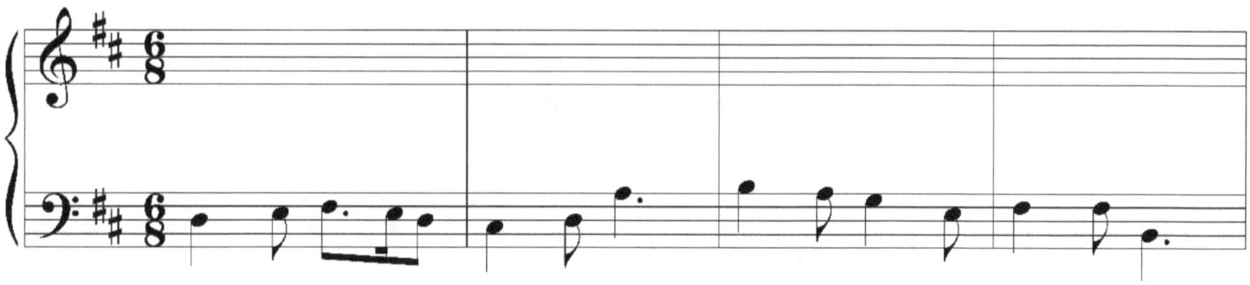

Numerals ______________________________

(b)

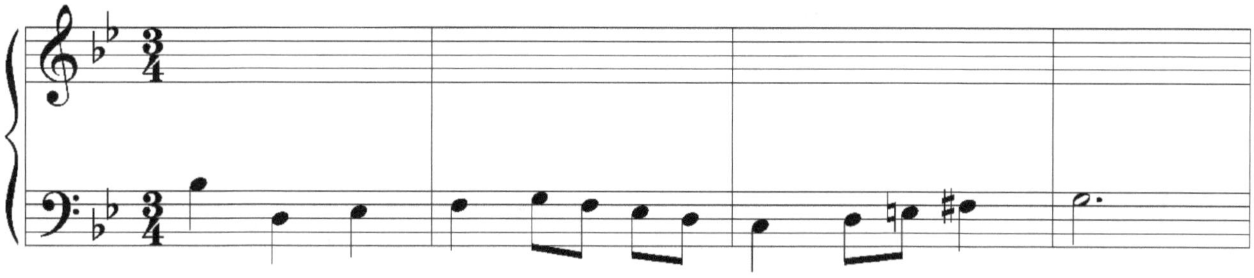

Numerals ______________________________

Working with a given soprano line

As always, when setting out to harmonise a given soprano line, the first step is to sing the given material to get a sense of the sound. Solfa will help you in this respect. If the new accidental is present in the given line this is a clear indication of the new key. Look at the cadence for confirmation.

Here is a worked example beginning in D major which modulates to the dominant.

Audio 5.5

Listen to the soprano line noting the effect of the accidental in bars 3 and 4.

It can be seen with the presence of G sharp in bars 3 and 4 that the key is changing to the dominant - A major.

The accidental G sharp is the leading note of A major, therefore the location of the pivot chord must occur earlier.

Let us extract the general area where we expect the pivot chord to be placed.

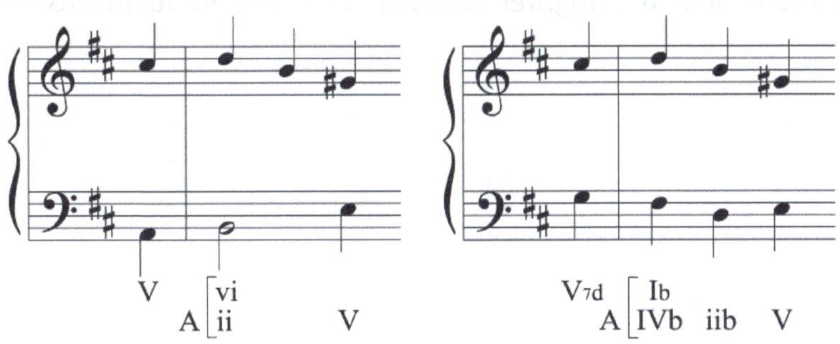

The above examples show two possible harmonisations with the pivot chord placed on the first beat of bar 3.

As mentioned earlier the sound of A major will only emerge when we hear the accidental G sharp. In terms of solfa it can be very helpful to change the doh position at this point; G sharp being the new leading note will now be sung as ***t***. This facilitates the identification of any cadential or melodic idioms that may appear with their associated harmonisations.

Now, back to the beginning to complete the bass line.

The final stage is to add parts for alto and tenor voices.

Audio 5.6

As you listen to the 4-part harmonisation notice the brighter sound as the music modulates to the sharp side of the key.

Here is a further example which begins in G major and modulates to its relative minor, E minor.

Audio 5.7

Sing along and add solfa as you listen to this short soprano phrase.

The key of E minor is clearly indicated by the presence of D sharp in bar 3. Therefore, the pivot chord must occur at an earlier point.

Let us extract the general area of bars 2 and 3 to find a suitable pivot location.

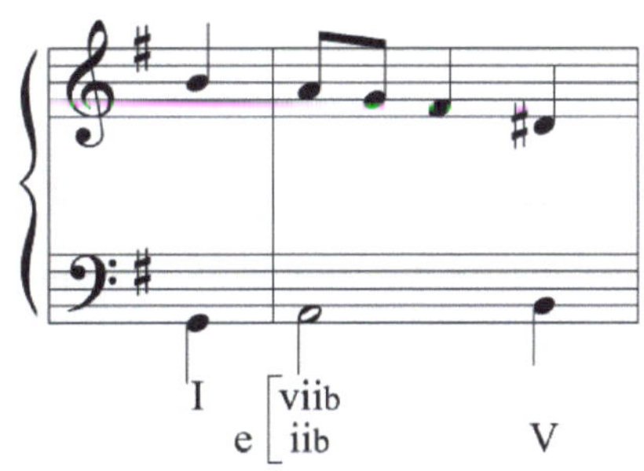

If the pivot chord is marked on the first beat of bar 3, the above examples show two possible harmonisations. However, the pivot chord could be placed a little earlier on the 3rd beat of bar 2, giving a further option below.

Remember the pivot chord may be marked on **any common** chord

Now back to the beginning to complete the bass line.

Option 1:

Option 2:

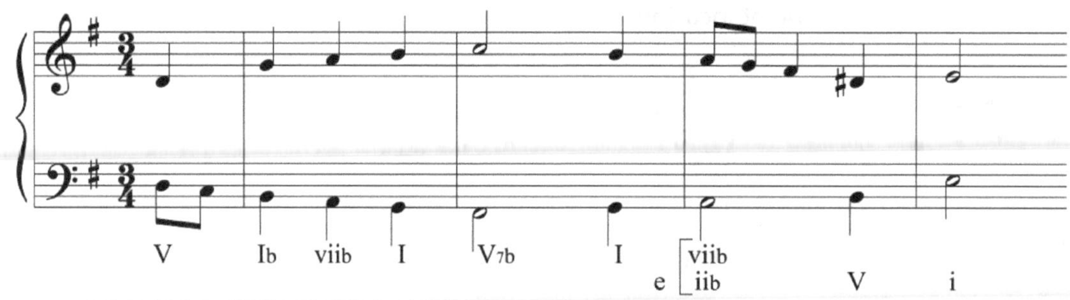

Option 3:

Here are each of the options complete with alto and tenor parts.

Option 1:

Audio 5.8

Listen to the first completed harmonisation.

Option 2:

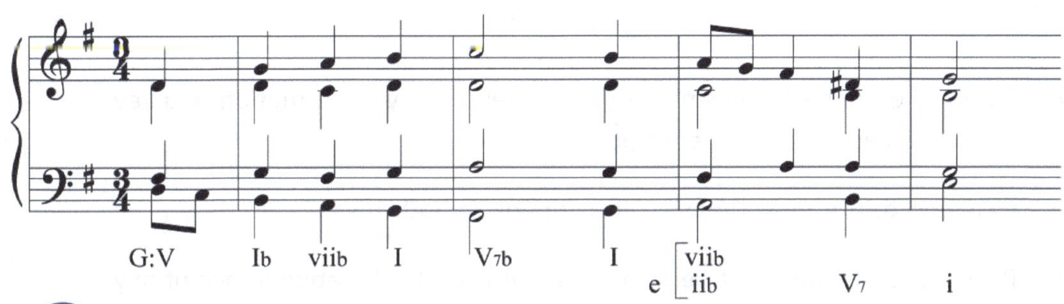

Audio 5.9

Listen to the alternative chord choices in option 2.

Option 3:

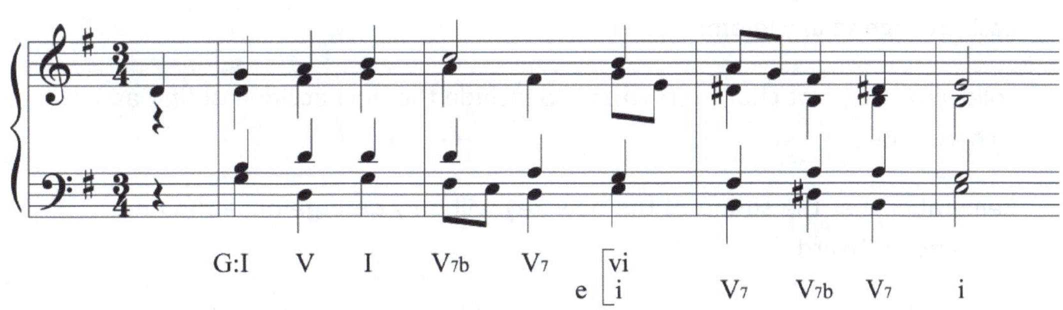

Audio 5.10

As you listen to the harmonisation in option 3, note the accidental is heard a little earlier in bar 3 as a chord note in the alto part.

The final step in the process is to look for the potential to add some further decoration to enhance the overall interest and musicality. Dissonant decoration is highlighted by the figured bass.

Here we explore Option 1.

Audio 5.11

Listening to the more active part writing you will appreciate the interest which the decoration creates.

Checklist✓

- Carefully examine the given material to identify any confirmation of a key change, especially at a cadence point
- Pivot chord: This must be mutually common to both keys
- Pivot location: This must be at some point prior to the appearance of any new accidentals
- Pivot labelling: This must show the roman numerals in relation to both keys
- Solfa will always help – it may be useful when moving from the tonic to dominant to change the ***doh*** position to think clearly in the new key and easily recognise any idioms
- Following the pivot chord remember to include the new accidental first as a chord note
- Remember that the sound of the new key will only emerge once the new accidental is heard
- Always aim for the most musical result possible. Interest and polish can be achieved with the addition of suitable decoration to the basic harmonisation

Exercise 5.5

Sing the given soprano line in each of the following exercises (solfa will be useful). Identify the key change. Begin by completing the bass line adding roman numerals. Then add inner voices. Finally explore possibilities for further decoration.

(a)

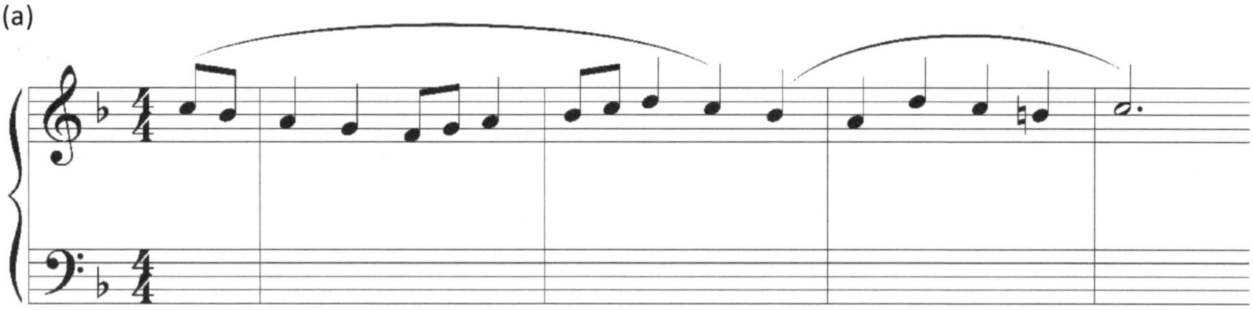

Numerals ______________________________

(b)

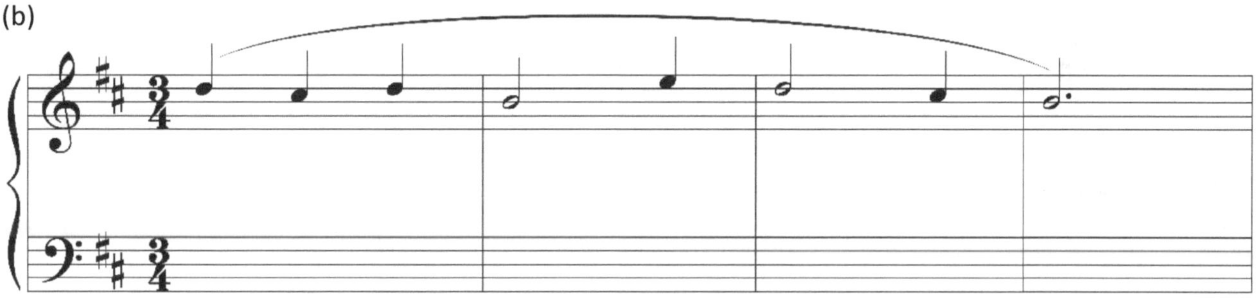

Numerals ______________________________

(c)

Numerals ______________________________

(d)

Numerals ______________________________

(e)

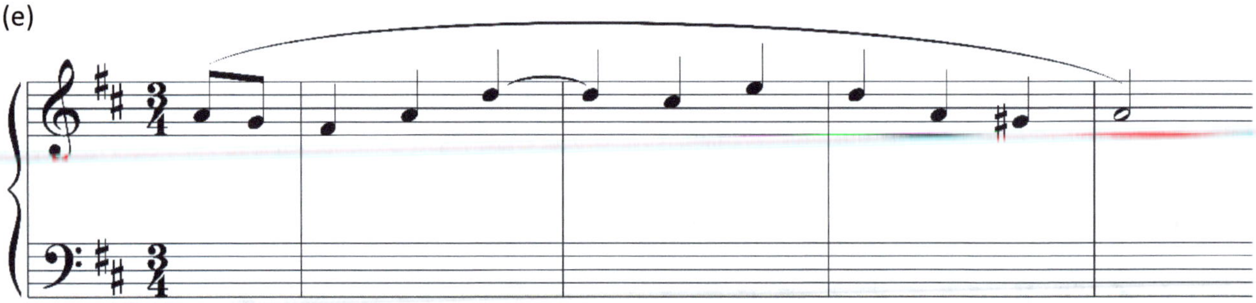

Numerals ______________________________

(f)

Numerals ______________________________

CHAPTER 6

MODULATION Part 2
Dominant and relative (minor keys)

Modulation from a minor key to its relative major

Audio 6.1

Listen to this extract from Beethoven's piano sonata in F minor Op. 2, No. 1. These are the opening bars of the third movement which begins in F minor and modulates to the relative major, A flat major, (from the third beat of bar 4 to the end of the extract).

Let us work through a bass line demonstrating a modulation from A minor to its relative – C major. The first step is to select all **common** chords between A minor and C major.

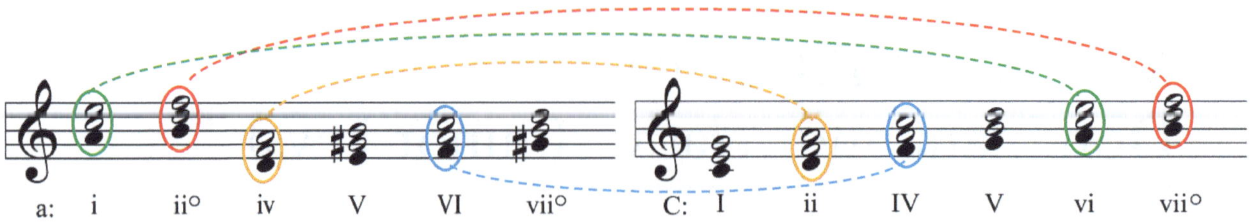

The colour matches show that there are 4 pivot chord options available between any minor key and its relative major.

Studying the bass line below and adding solfa, we notice the presence of G natural (***s***) in bar 3 which clearly denotes the move to C major confirmed by the perfect cadence. Therefore, the pivot chord must occur in advance of the G natural (***s***).

This bass offers a few choices at which the pivot chord may be marked as follows:

Although we have marked the pivot chord in several different locations, the **sound** of the progressions remains the same.

When moving from a minor key to its **relative major** the 'accidental' may be less apparent as ***si*** reverts to ***s*** i.e., an accidental sign will not always be needed.

Now we complete the harmonisation adding the soprano line first followed by alto and tenor parts.

Audio 6.2

First you will hear both outer lines followed by the full 4-part harmonisation.

Exercise 6.1

In these exercises the location of the pivot chord has been marked. Each new key is established with a perfect cadence. Add roman numerals, then add alto and tenor parts.

(a)

Numerals ______________________________

(b)

Numerals ______________________________

Exercise 6.2

Each bass line begins in a minor key, sing it using solfa. The presence of *s* will indicate the new key. Label the bass carefully deciding a suitable location for the pivot chord. Complete the soprano line followed by alto and tenor parts.

(a)

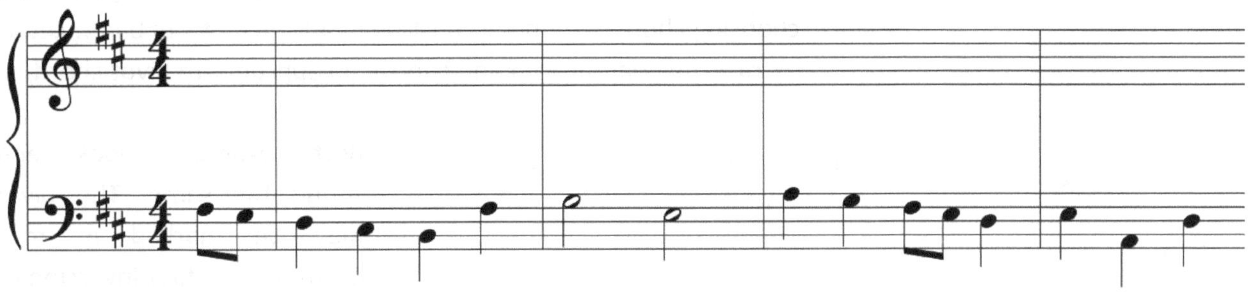

Numerals ______________________________

(b)

Numerals ______________________________

Next is a worked example harmonising a simple melody beginning in D minor.

As we sing the melody using solfa the presence of ***s*** followed by the octave leap in bar 3 creates a strong move to F major. When choosing chords, the pivot must be in advance of ***s*** in bar 3. Let us extract the general area and choose an appropriate pivot chord.

Both examples look and sound the same. The pivot may be marked in root position or in first inversion of the same chord in bar 2.

Remember this will not change the actual **sound** of the harmony but rather pinpoint where the thinking turns in the direction of the new key.

Now to complete the bass line.

The final step is to include alto and tenor parts.

Audio 6.3

First you will hear the soprano and bass lines followed by the full 4-part harmonisation.

Here is a further example of a melody in D minor with a modulation to F major. Sing using solfa.

The location of the pivot chord must be in the area following ***si*** and before ***s*** i.e., bar 3.

Let us explore the harmonic possibilities of bar 3.

There are 3 different pivot chord options all equally viable. Remember that the new key (F major) is not audible until ***s*** in the melody is **harmonised** in bar 4.

Notice, in all the options shown, we have included a passing note ***s***, on the 2nd quaver of beat 2. This is correct in the context of D minor and does not yet indicate F major.

Now let us complete the bass part. In this instance we have selected beat 3 in bar 3 to act as the pivot chord.

Audio 6.4

Listen to the completed soprano and bass lines.

The final step is to add alto and tenor parts. The examples below show two different possibilities in the detail of the part writing.

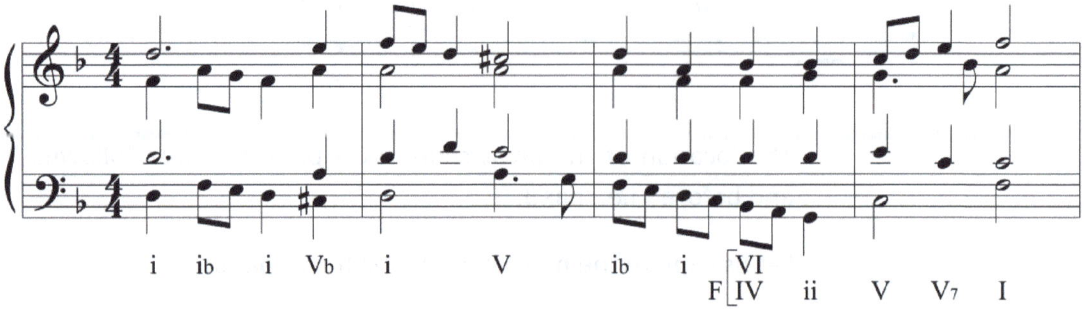

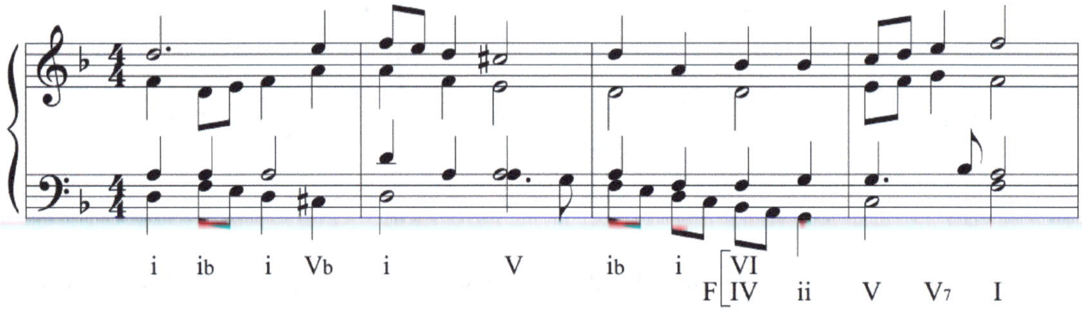

Audio 6.5

You may wish to listen to the full harmonisation several times to compare the different shaping of the inner parts.

Exercise 6.3

Sing the given soprano line in each of the following exercises. Solfa will be useful. Identify the key change and decide an appropriate pivot chord. Complete the bass line adding roman numerals, then add inner voices. Finally explore possibilities for some further decoration.

(a)

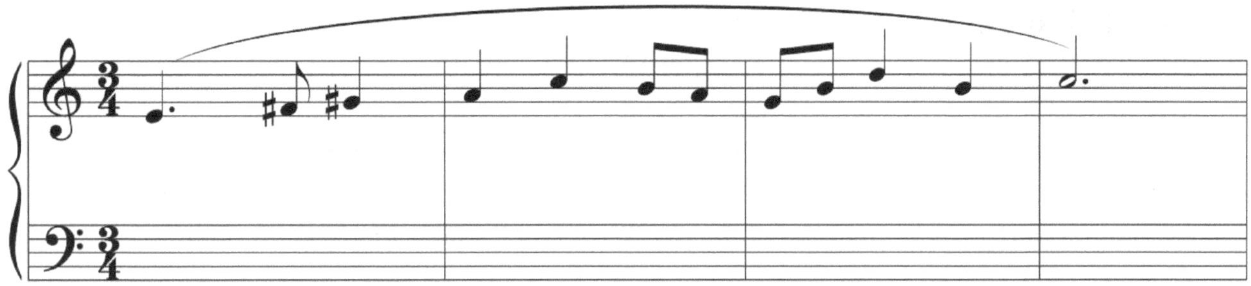

Numerals ____

(b)

Numerals ____

(c)

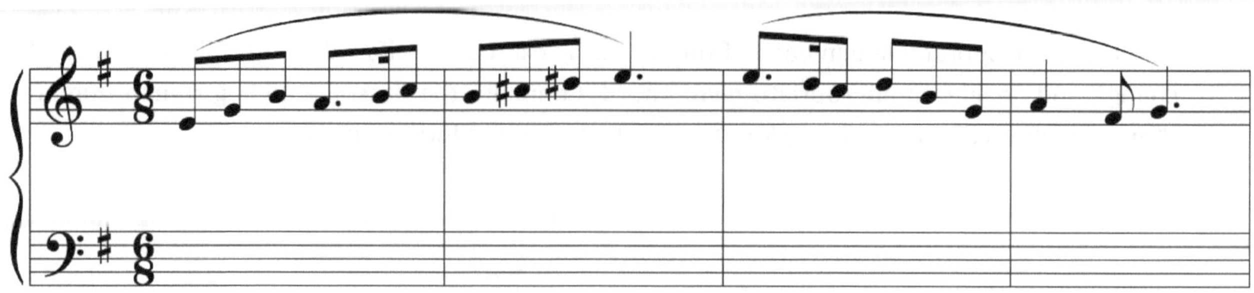

Numerals ____

(d)

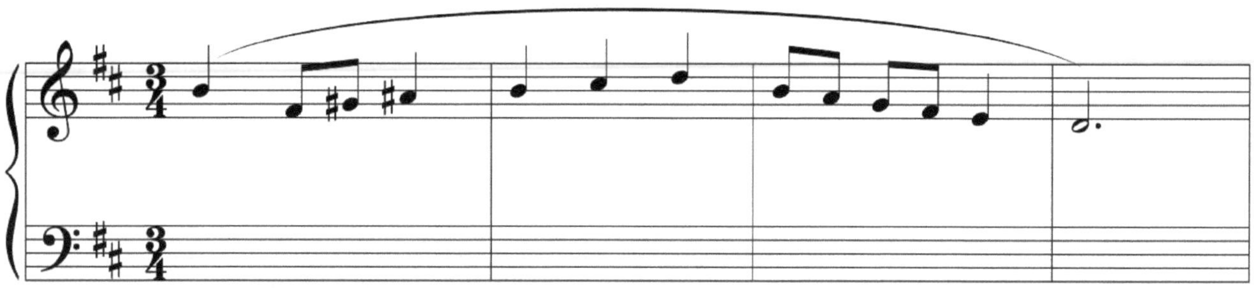

Numerals ____

Modulation from a minor key to its dominant

Audio 6.6

Listen to this extract from the opening bars of Schumann's *'The Stranger'* from his Album for the Young Op. 68. The music begins in D minor and modulates to the dominant key of A minor, ending the short section with a perfect cadence in the new key.

Let us work an example demonstrating a modulation from A minor to E minor. The first step is to select all common chords between A minor and E minor.

It can now be seen that there is only one pivot chord available.

In the following example there is opportunity to mark the pivot chord on either beats 1 or 2 in bar 3. Then, thinking ahead in the new key the roman numerals show the chosen harmonisation for the remainder.

We continue by completing the soprano line first, making sure to include all the appropriate accidentals.

While adding alto and tenor parts we avail of opportunities to include some decoration for added interest which is highlighted by the figured bass.

Audio 6.7

Listen first to the outer lines, then the full 4-part harmonisation with suspension decoration added in the inner parts.

> A modulation from a minor key to its dominant has only one common chord. Chord **i** in the tonic key becomes chord **iv** in the dominant key.

Exercise 6.4

Label each bass line carefully deciding a location for the pivot chord. The new key is established with a perfect cadence. Complete the soprano line followed by alto and tenor parts. Remember to include all necessary accidentals.

(a)

Numerals ____

(b)

Numerals ____

(c)

Numerals ____

Next is a worked example harmonising a simple melody beginning in G minor.

As we sing the melody the presence in bar 3 of B natural and C sharp indicates a move to D minor.

You may find it useful when using solfa to change the ***d*** position at the beginning of bar 3: the pitch A becomes a new ***m***. This facilitates the identification of a strong cadential feature establishing D minor.

When choosing chords, the pivot must be located in advance of the new accidentals in bar 3.

As already indicated, there is only one pivot chord available between a minor key and its dominant; namely chord **i** in the tonic key becoming chord **iv** in the dominant key.

In this instance, the G minor tonic chord is clearly suggested in bar 2.

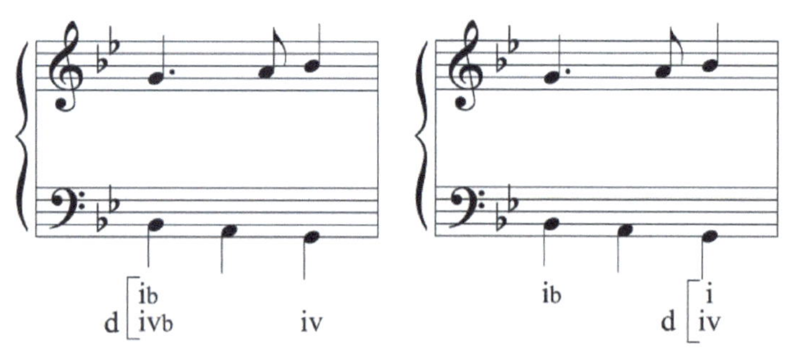

The first inversion or the root position of the chord may be marked as the pivot.

Now to complete the bass line.

The final step is to include alto and tenor parts taking care to include all new accidentals.

Audio 6.8

Listen first to the soprano and bass lines, then hear the full 4-part harmonisation.

Exercise 6.5

Sing or play each melody. Look for an appropriate place to use the original tonic chord which will act as the pivot to the dominant key. Complete the bass line followed by inner voices. Finally consider some additional decoration.

(a)

Numerals ____

(b)

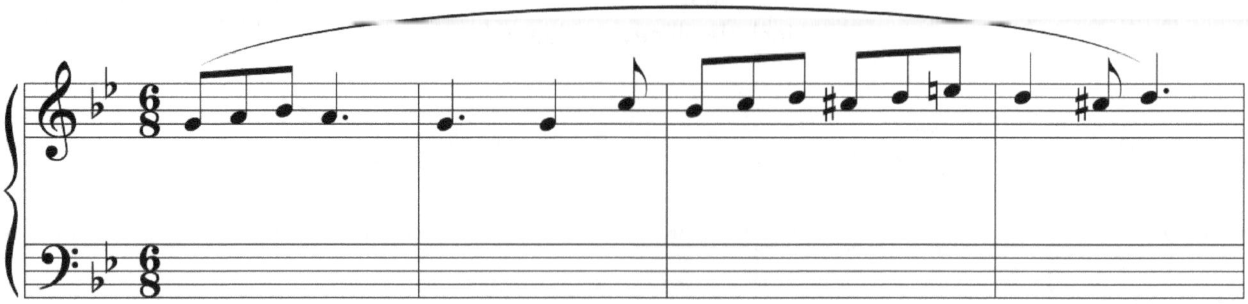

Numerals ______________________________

(c)

Numerals ______________________________

CHAPTER 7

MODULATION Part 3
Transition

Another method of modulating is to change directly to a new key by means of chromatic movement. This is an abrupt change called transition and is often used for a brief modulation.

Let us examine this bass line.

Notice the chromatic movement in bar 3; the F sharp introduces the key of G major.

A significant feature of transition is how the **new** accidental is harmonised. The chord with the strongest character is **V** or **V7** and this most effectively harmonises the new accidental in any appropriate position.

It can be clearly seen that **no** pivot chord is used in transition; the use of a line indicates the direct shift to the new key. This has the effect of an abrupt change making the new tonality immediately apparent.

To this bass we add a possible soprano line.

Finally, alto and tenor parts complete the harmonisation.

Audio 7.1

Listen first to the soprano and bass lines, followed by the complete harmonisation. As you listen, focus on the chromatic movement in the bass line.

Here is a soprano melody demonstrating transition.

Notice the chromatic movement in bar 3; the G sharp introduces the key of A minor which is best harmonised as part of **V** or **V7.**

Now we add a bass line.

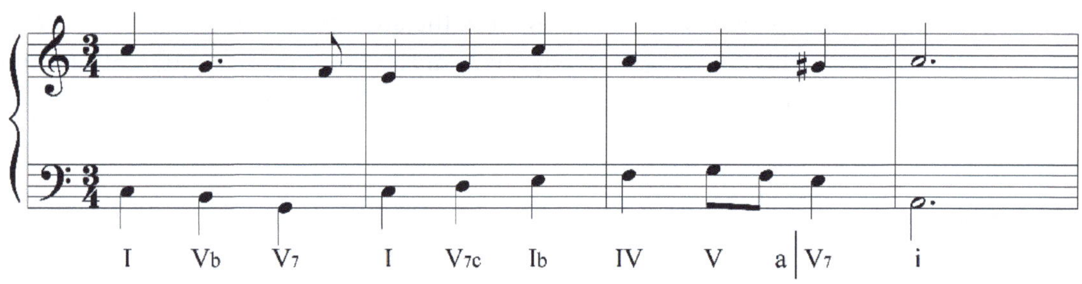

Finally, alto and tenor parts complete the harmonisation.

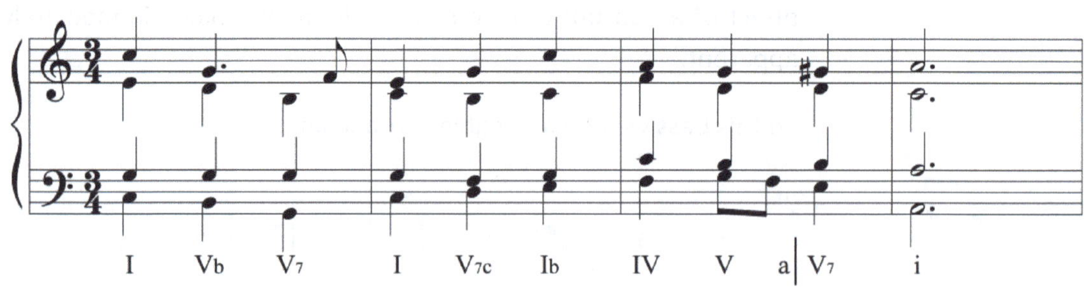

Audio 7.2

First, listen to the soprano and bass lines followed by the full 4-part harmonisation.

To date, a new key has been confirmed by a perfect cadence. However, in the example below you will see that this need not always be the case.

This melody begins in E minor and has a chromatic move C – C sharp in bar 2. C sharp may indicate either the key of D major or B minor and looking ahead to the A sharp in bar 4, the key of B minor is the obvious choice.

Now we add a bass line.

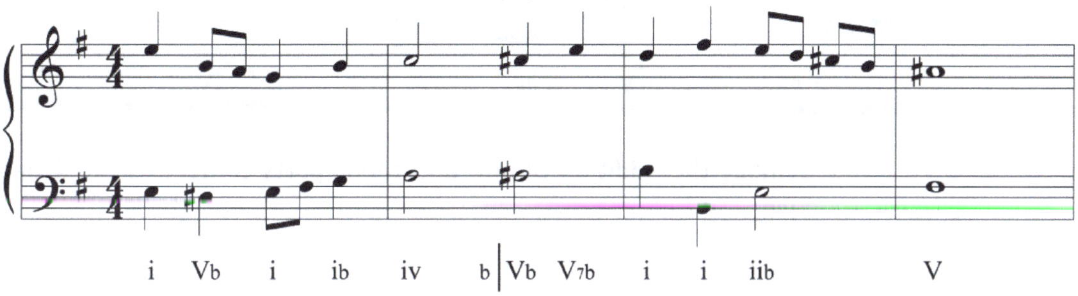

Notice the new key of B minor has been strongly established even though the phrase ends with an imperfect cadence.

Next, the harmonisation is completed by adding inner voices.

Audio 7.3

First you hear the outer lines – notice a simultaneous chromatic movement in both soprano and bass parts. The 4-part harmonisation that follows gives the full effect of the modulation albeit ending with a half close.

This melody begins in G minor and modulates to D minor through the chromatic shift C to C sharp in bar 2.

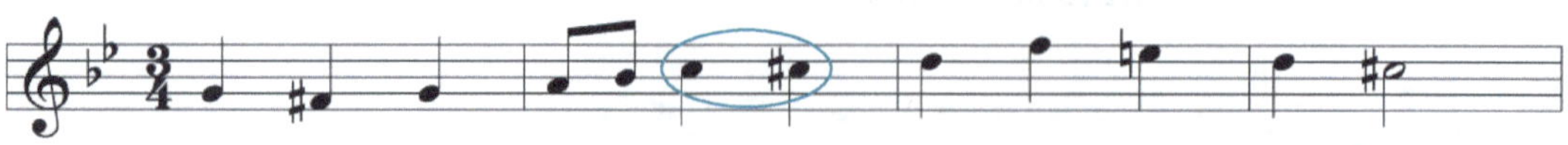

The added bass line demonstrates the use of **V7c** as the chord of transition.

Finally the addition of alto and tenor parts completes the 4-part harmonisation.

Audio 7.4

You will hear the outer lines first followed by the full 4-part harmonisation. The shift to the dominant key creates a brighter effect being on the sharp side of the key.

Checklist✓

- A chromatic move indicates a transition
- This chromatic move should occur in the same voice
- The chord which harmonises the new accidental should be the dominant/dominant 7th of the new key
- The dominant/dominant 7th transition chord can be used in root position or in any inversion
- A minor key modulation to its dominant has two accidentals – the crucial one being the new leading note

Exercise 7.1

Following the given figured bass add roman numerals identifying the point of modulation. Add alto and tenor parts.

(a)

Numerals ______________________________

(b)

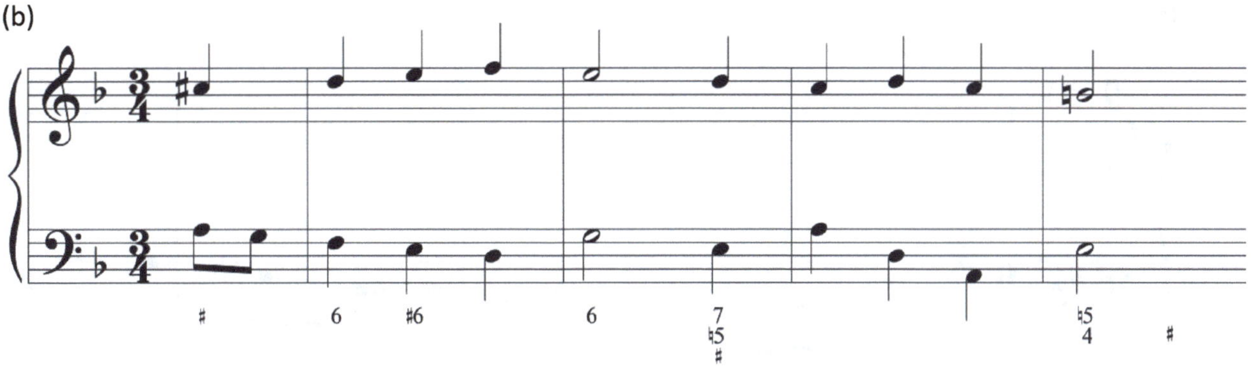

Numerals ______________________________

Exercise 7.2

Add roman numerals to show your chosen harmonisation for the following bass lines. Then add a soprano melody and finally complete parts for alto and tenor voices. Take care with accidentals.

(a)

Numerals ____

(b)

Numerals ____

(c)

Numerals ____

Exercise 7.3

Sing or play each melody. Identify the point of modulation and complete a bass line. Finally, add alto and tenor parts.

(a)

Numerals ____

(b)

Numerals ____

(c)

Numerals ____

CHAPTER 8

MODULATION Part 4

Pivot. Transition. Home key.

This chapter draws together all elements of modulation studied so far and includes a return to the tonic key. Our modulation options at present are to the relative and to the dominant keys.

To begin, we will work through a bass line step-by-step.

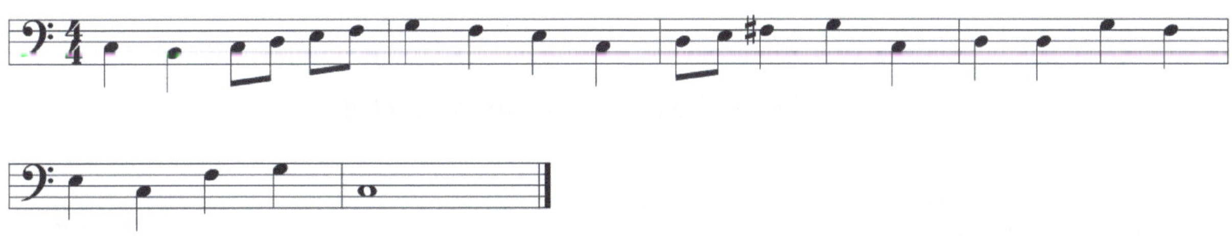

In this C major bass line, a modulation to G major is indicated by F sharp in bar 3, while the presence of F natural in bar 4 shows a return to the tonic key.

In selecting the harmonies, we see that pivot chords are possible for both the move to G major and the return to the tonic key.

The next step is to add a shapely soprano line – always being aware of any new accidentals.

Finally, alto and tenor parts are added.

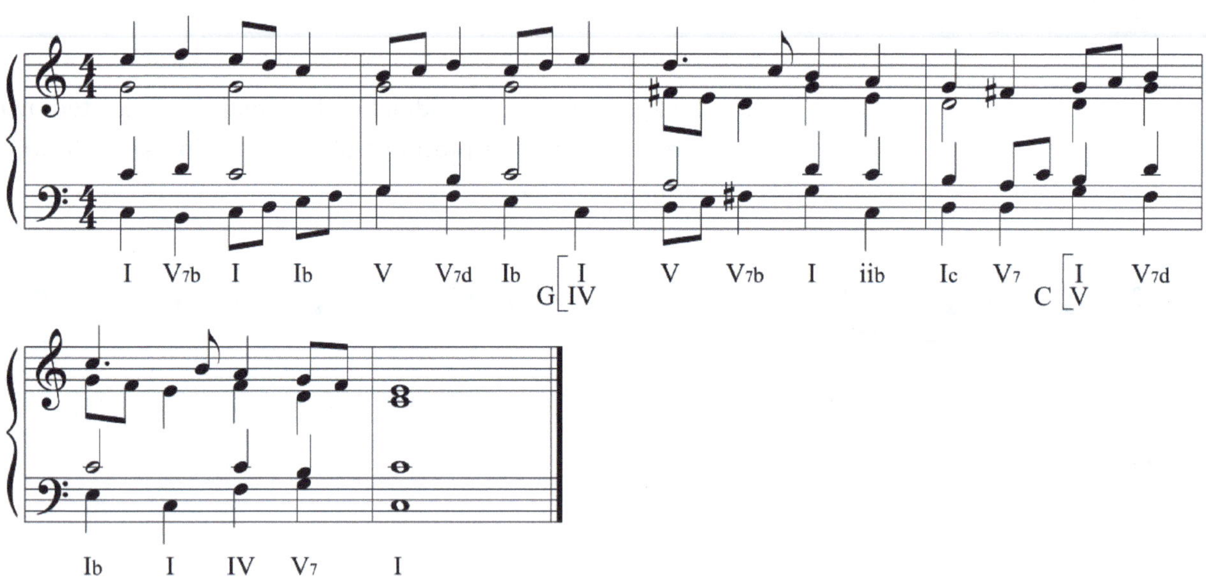

Audio 8.1

Begin by listening to the bass line alone, then the soprano and bass parts together and finally the complete 4-part harmonisation.

The next example of a bass line shows both transition and pivot.

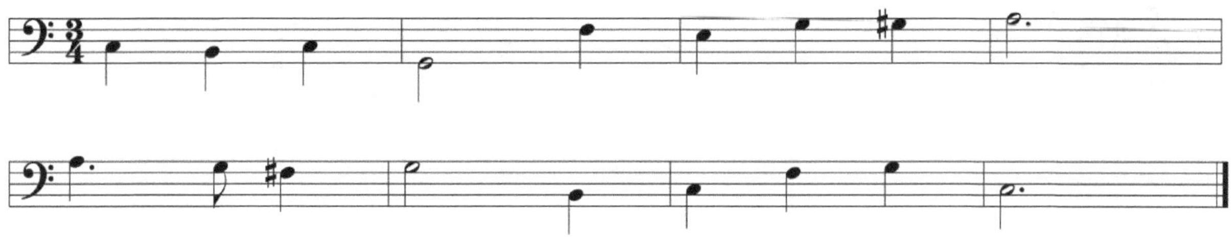

Beginning in C major the chromatic move from G to G sharp in bar 3 creates a brief transition to A minor while the F sharp in bar 5 indicates a change to G major before returning home to the tonic.

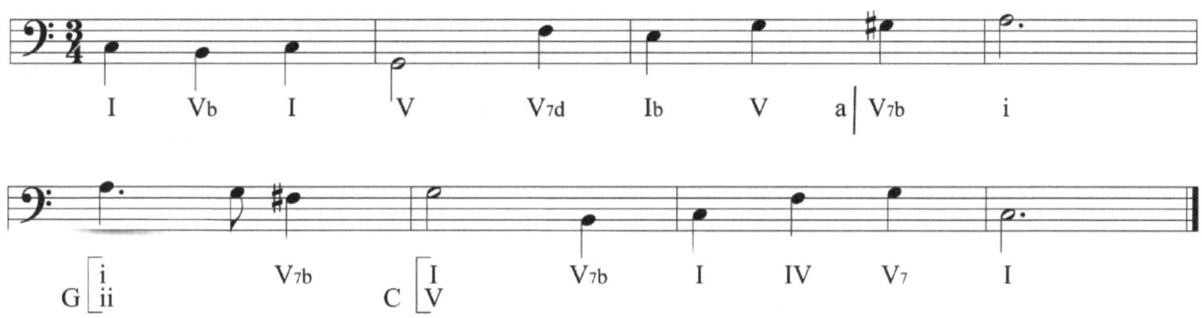

As we choose the chords, the transition chord on G sharp in bar 3 must be the dominant/dominant 7th of the new key.

The first chord in bar 5 functions as a pivot into G major while the G major chord in bar 6 acts as an obvious pivot returning to the tonic.

Now a shapely soprano line is added.

Finally, parts for alto and tenor complete the harmonisation.

Audio 8.2

Begin by listening to the bass line alone, then the soprano and bass parts together and finally the complete 4-part harmonisation which has additional interest in the detail of the part writing.

Exercise 8.1

Study the given soprano and bass lines. Add roman numerals according to the figured bass and indicate any key changes. Complete the harmonisation by adding inner voices. Always be aware of necessary accidentals.

(a)

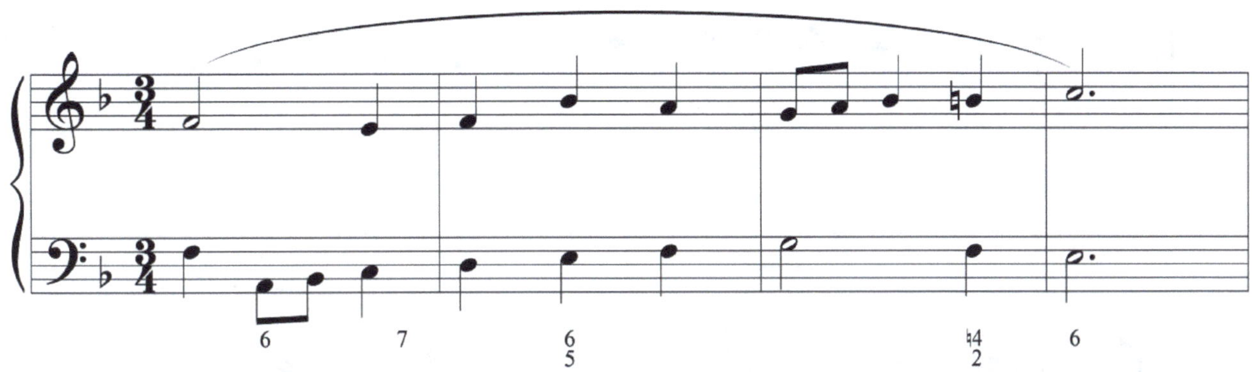

Numerals ____

____

(b)

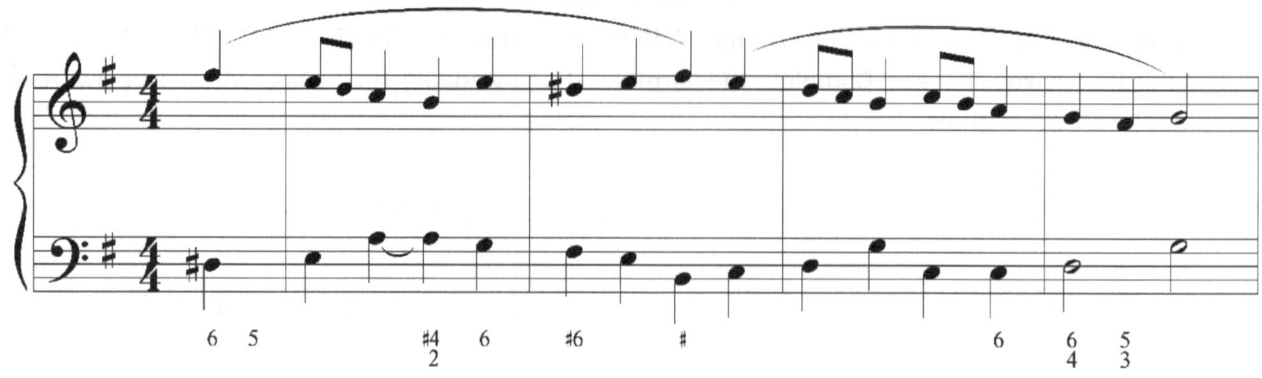

Numerals ____

____

(c)

Numerals ____

____

(d)

Numerals ____

____

Sing or play this melody in A minor. A definite modulation to E minor is indicated by the end of the first phrase. Although there are no apparent accidentals in the second phrase, a further key change could be explored.

In choosing a bass line, let us begin with the simplest option – moving to E minor by the end of the first phrase and returning to the home key for all of the second phrase.

Now to work out the detail of the chords and the bass line:

The second half of bar 2 is an appropriate pivot into E minor which is confirmed with a perfect cadence at the end of the phrase.

At the beginning of bar 5 the same pivot chord is used as an effective return to the tonic.

The addition of alto and tenor parts completes the harmonisation.

Audio 8.3

Listen to the 3 steps of the harmonisation above.

Let us re-examine the second phrase to explore a further tonality - a move to C major before returning to the tonic key of A minor.

The beginning of phrase 2 offers strong chord choices to make an effective move to C major, whilst the beginning of bar 7 facilitates a return to the tonic.

Alto and tenor parts can now be added.

Audio 8.4

First you will hear the soprano and bass parts alone, then the SATB harmonisation gives the full effect of the tonal changes.

Audio 8.5

Finally, listen once more to compare both SATB versions. Although each is strong, the second example provides more tonal colour.

Before completing the final set of exercises review the following points:

Checklist✓

- Sing or play all given material
- Accidentals in the given line make modulations easily recognisable
- When no accidentals are apparent a modulation may still be possible
- Both pivot and transition methods may be utilised in the one harmonisation

Exercise 8.2

Sing or play the given melodies, examining each for possible modulations. Add a strong bass line including roman numerals. Finally, add inner voices. Remember, necessary accidentals are vital!

(a)

Numerals ______________________________

____

(b)

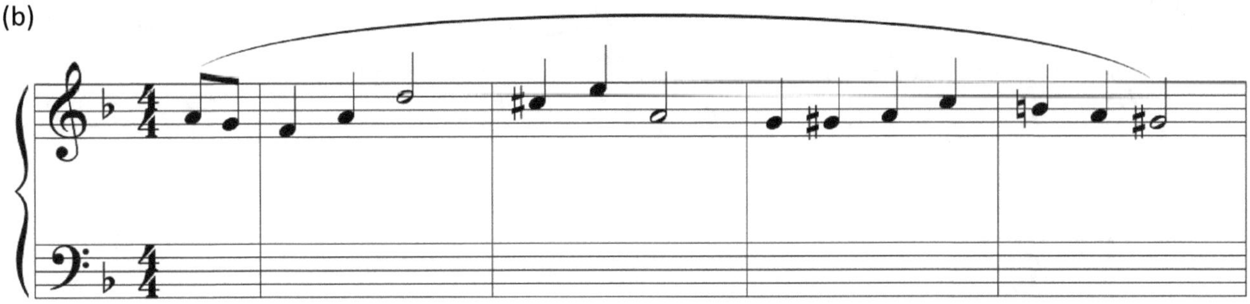

Numerals

(c)

Numerals

(d)

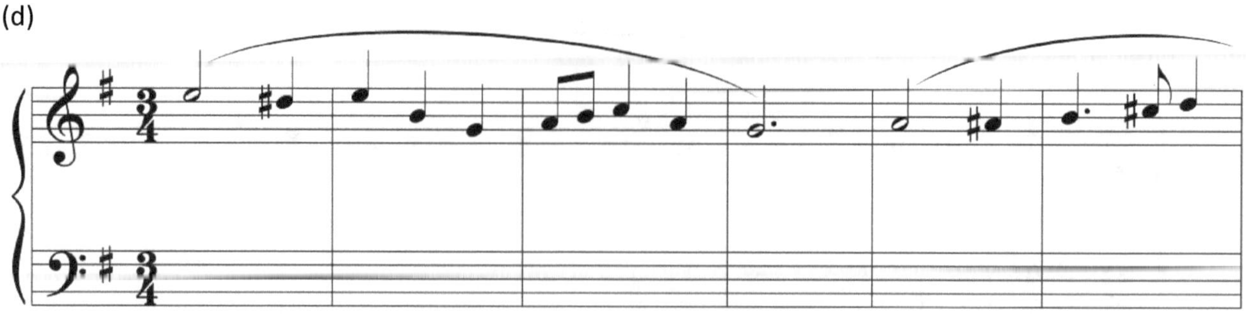

Numerals

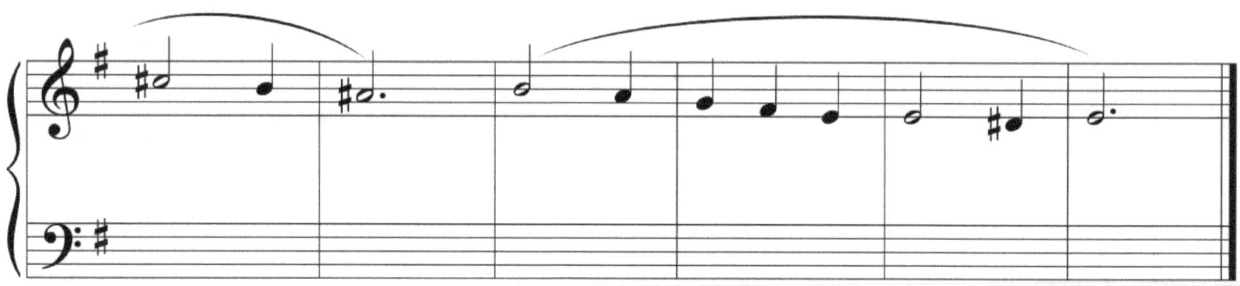

CHAPTER 9

MODULATION Part 5
Expanding the range of keys

Here is a reminder of the full range of closely related keys.

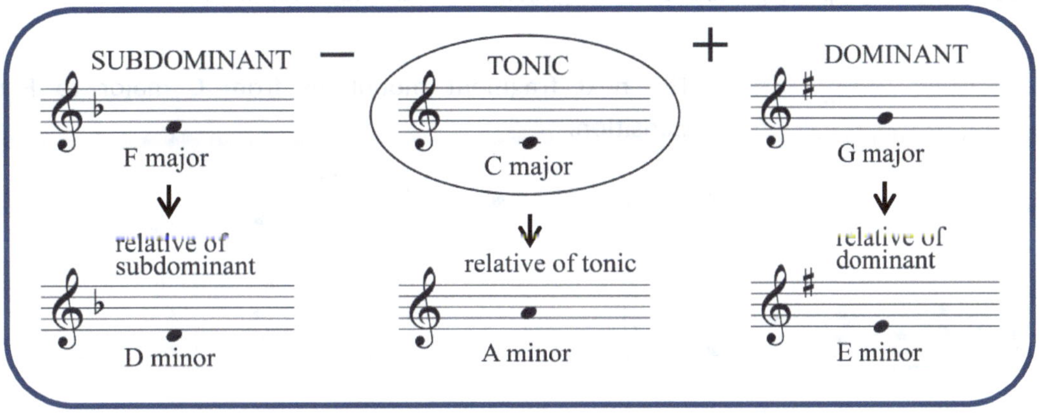

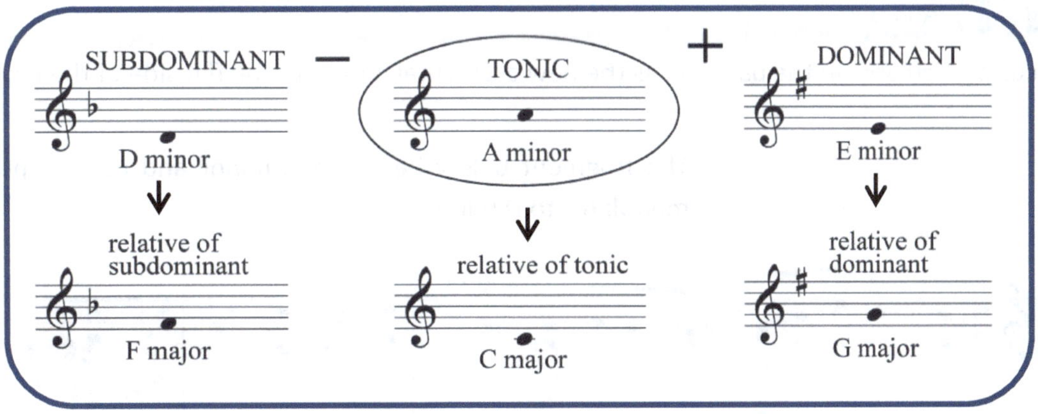

Study the short SATB passages that follow to hear a variety of modulations exploring the full range of related keys. The fragments demonstrate both pivot and transition as a method of modulating.

This short fragment modulates from C major to E minor by means of a pivot chord.

Audio 9.1

As you listen to the passage above, try singing along with the outer lines.

The next fragment modulates from C major to F major by transition.

Audio 9.2

Focus particularly on the bass line as the new accidental moves to the flat side of the key.

The fragment below begins in A minor and using a pivot chord modulates to D minor.

Audio 9.3

Notice that the tone becomes somewhat darker when the key centre moves to the subdominant.

This fragment begins in A minor and modulates by transition to G major.

Audio 9.4

Notice that the transition chord in bar 3 lifts the tonality to a much brighter realm.

Exercise 9.1

Study the given soprano and bass lines. Add roman numerals according to the figured bass. Complete the harmonisation by adding alto and tenor parts.

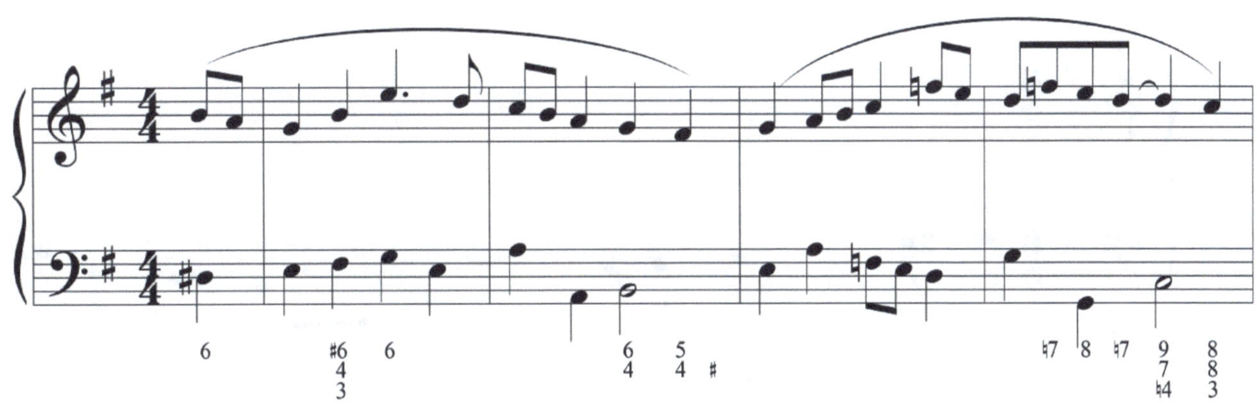

Numerals ____

Exercise 9.2

Add roman numerals as implied by the given soprano and bass lines. Add inner parts to complete the harmonisation being mindful of necessary accidentals.

Numerals ____

Exercise 9.3

Study the given bass and identify the key change. Choose appropriate chording and add roman numerals. Write a shapely soprano line and finally add inner voices.

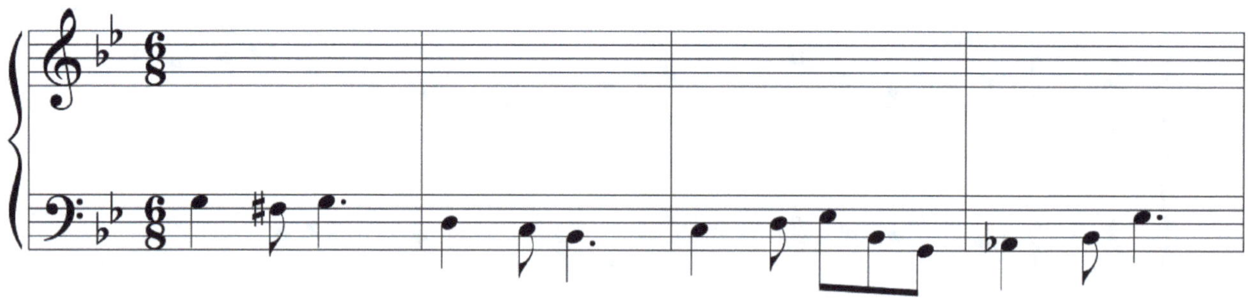

Numerals ____

Exercise 9.4

Sing or play the given soprano lines noting the accidentals and key change. Begin by choosing basic chords. Take time to review and refine chord positions in order to craft a well shaped bass line. Finally, complete each harmonisation by adding parts for alto and tenor voices.

(a)

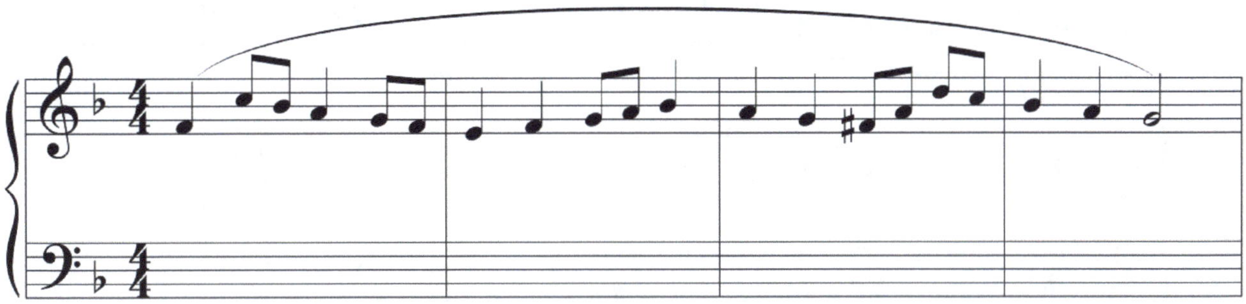

Numerals ____

(b)

Numerals ____

Longer phrases with further modulation and returning to the tonic

Audio 9.5

Listen to *Allegro in F,* No. 2 from '12 Easy Pieces' by Haydn. The commentary below outlines the key changes during the course of the piece.

The music begins in F major and modulates to C major (dominant) in bars 7 and 8. The upbeat to bar 9 modulates to G minor (relative of the subdominant) followed by a sequence in the next 2 bars (upbeat to bar 11) modulating back to F major. A further move to C major is made from bars 17 – 22 while the tonic is re-established from bar 23. A glimpse of B flat major (subdominant) is included at the end of bar 30 into the start of bar 31. Thereafter, the music reaffirms and ends in the tonic key.

A more extended harmonisation which may include several modulations and a return to the tonic key can be approached in the following way as a method of working.

- Identify the tonic key and map out the range of 5 related keys.
- Sing any given material.
- Look for accidentals and cadence points to help identify main key changes – these are most likely to be approached by pivot.
- Further glimpses of tonal colour may be included – often by transition.
- Always expect a return to the tonic key to end the piece.

This F major harmonisation follows the suggested order of working.

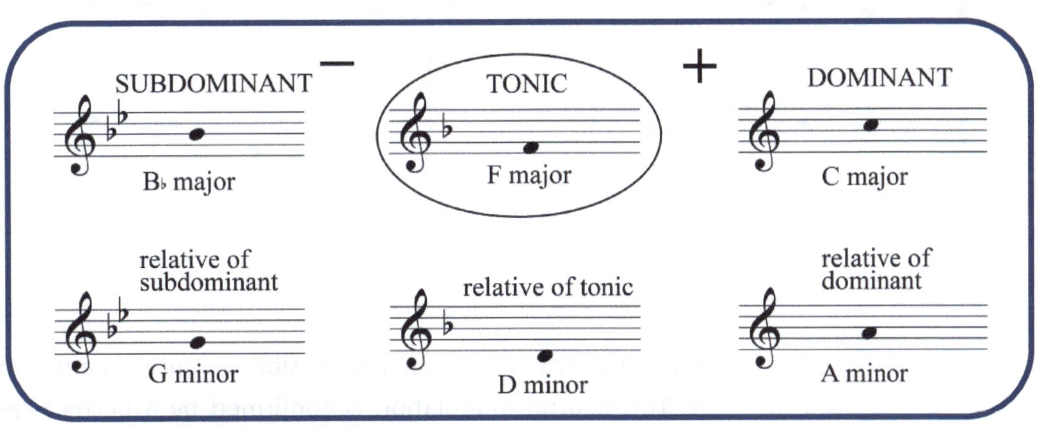

Sing the given material and explore the possible key options.

The first phrase clearly establishes the tonic key moving towards an imperfect cadence in bar 2.

In the second phrase the B natural in bar 4 clearly indicates a modulation to C major concluding with a perfect cadence.

Further accidentals are presented in bars 5 and 6 suggesting the keys of G minor and A minor respectively. Notice the same bass shaping which creates a sequence. A sequence is a useful technique allowing for other keys to appear in quick succession.

The final 2 bars see a return to the tonic.

Let us now sketch a possible bass for bars 1 – 4.

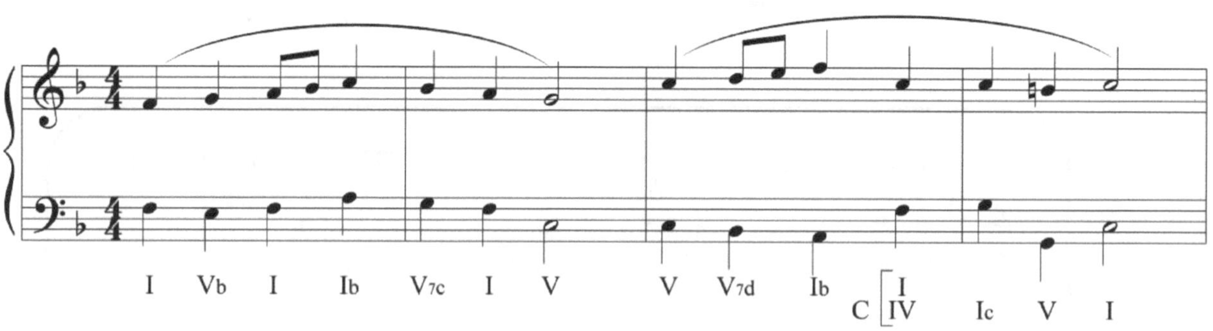

A pivot chord into C major is possible in bar 3 on either beat 3 or 4. This central modulation is confirmed by a perfect cadence in bar 4.

Now to analyse the chording suggested by the given bass.

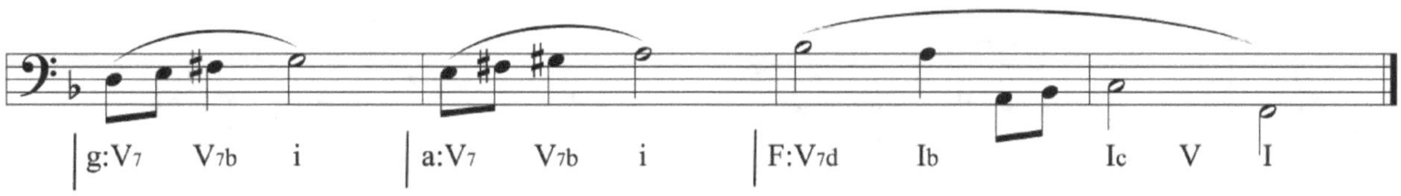

Bar 5 outlines dominant and tonic chords in G minor.

Similiarly bar 6 also outlines dominant and tonic chords in A minor.

A feature of modulating sequence is to mimic the same chordal progressions in different keys. In this case transition is used for each of the key changes.

Bar 7 also uses dominant and tonic chords (though not in sequential shape) to give a strong return to the tonic key.

Let us now complete the soprano line through the second half of the piece.

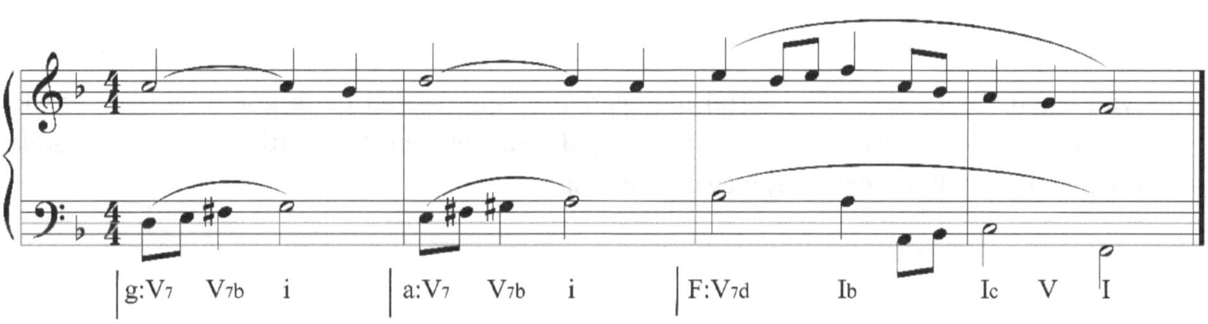

As bars 5 and 6 use a harmonic sequence, it is recommended that a melodic sequence is also crafted in the soprano line. This strengthens the overall impact of the sequence.

Bar 7 continues the rising profile of the soprano line to reach the high F which then relaxes downwards to the final cadence.

To complete the harmonisation alto and tenor parts are added.

Audio 9.6

As you listen, notice how the central modulation is approached quite gradually, whereas the modulating sequence that follows creates a rapid shift between two further keys. Some added interest in the detail is supplied by way of suspensions.

This minor key harmonisation also follows the suggested pattern of working.

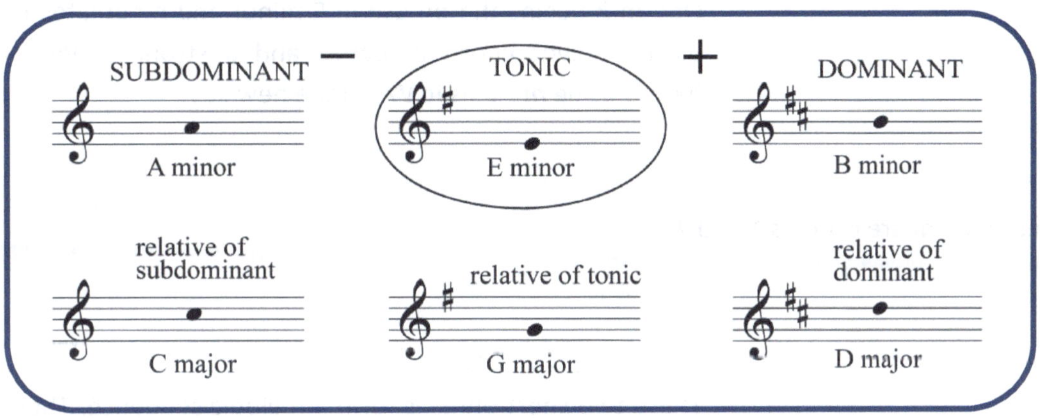

Sing or play the melody watching out for accidentals.

Look carefully at phrase endings which most likely suggest possible modulations and/or sequential activity.

Note the expected return to the tonic.

Bars 1 – 4:

Looking at the first phrase; there are no apparent accidentals and the solfa in bars 3 and 4 being ***m f m r d*** will allow a harmonisation in either E minor or G major.

Here are possible bass lines showing these two options:

Option 1

In this instance, the phrase remains in E minor, using chords **V** and **V7b** with a passing note C sharp (melodic minor), which gives both flow and colour to reach the tonic chord at the end of the phrase.

Option 2

Option 2 begins the phrase in E minor and modulates to G major using a pivot chord in bar 2 and a strong cadential feature harmonising ***m r d*** as **Ic V7 I** in the new key.

Audio 9.7

Listen to compare options 1 and 2.

Up-beat to bars 5 & 6:

These two short phrases form a melodic sequence. There are two options. Firstly, the G sharp indicates the key of A minor and if we disregard the sequence, there being no further accidentals, we could continue to harmonise in A minor as in option 1.

Option 1

Secondly, fully recognising the potential of sequence, we can explore two key areas – A minor and C major with strong dominant and tonic harmony in each, as in option 2.

Option 2

The second harmonisation is more effective, giving a modulating sequence in which the bass shape of the first pattern in A minor is mimicked in the second pattern in C major.

Notice the bass in bar 5 takes a leap of a 7th – at this point in the harmonisation the aim is to highlight and preserve the sequential feature, therefore the bass leap in bar 7 is acceptable. Whilst the aim is to preserve the sequential shape in the outer voices, the inner voices may be freer.

Audio 9.8

Compare options 1 and 2. The modulating sequence in option 2 is musically more interesting.

Up-beat to bar 7:
The D sharp at the start of the final phrase indicates a return to the tonic key with prominent dominant and tonic harmony.

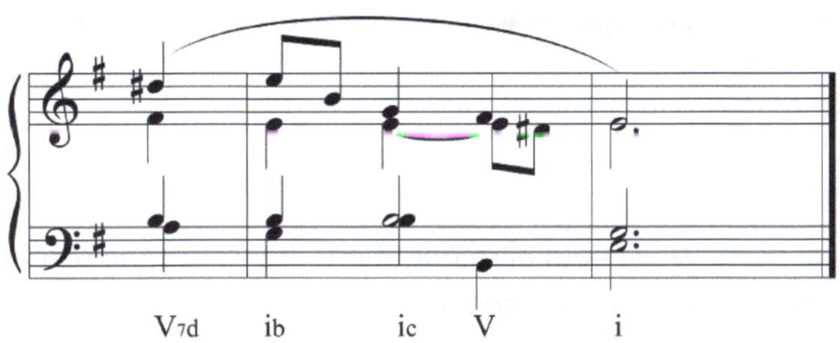

The final step is to add inner voices in each option.

Option 1:

Option 2:

Audio 9.9

Listen carefully to both options for comparison. While both harmonisations are viable, the second option offers more interest in its exploration of greater tonal colour.

Before completing the set of exercises that follow, review the following points:

Checklist✓

- Play/sing all given material carefully
- Identify the tonic key and plot out the 5 closely related keys
- Make a special note of each new leading note in relation to these keys
- Examine cadence points and any given accidentals to help identify main key changes
- Both pivot and transition are likely
- Watch out for modulating sequences – remember these are based around dominant/dominant 7th and tonic chords in the relevant keys
- An effective sequence will preserve the pattern in soprano and bass parts, while inner voices may be free
- When no accidentals are apparent, a modulation may still be possible, providing more tonal interest
- Expect a return to the tonic key for the final cadence
- As a final step, where appropriate, review the harmonisation to assess if further decoration would enhance the overall interest

Exercise 9.5

Carefully study the given material noting the various modulations. Add inner voices taking care with accidentals.

Numerals ____

____

Exercise 9.6

Carefully study the given material. Add roman numerals according to the figured bass, noting the modulations. Complete by adding inner voices.

Numerals ____

____

Exercise 9.7

In the exercises below study the given lines. Be mindful of accidentals to help identify changes of key. In particular, note the modulating sequences in the second system. Complete the outer lines before adding inner voices.

(a)

Numerals ______________________________

____

(b)

Numerals

Exercise 9.8

Study the bass line. Note the likely modulation at the central cadence. Identify the keys in the modulating sequence and when crafting the soprano line in this area be sure to compliment the sequential feature. Now complete the entire soprano line and finally add parts for alto and tenor voices.

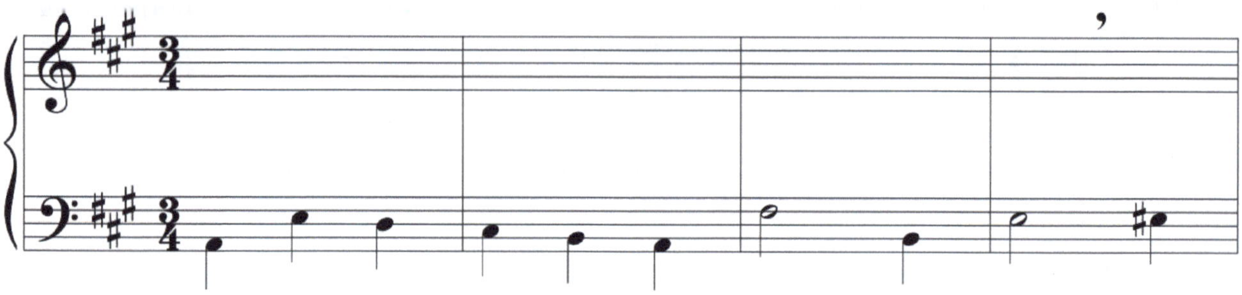

Numerals ____

Exercise 9.9

Sing/play the soprano line noting all accidentals. Identify the modulations and any sequences. Complete a strong bass line, phrase by phrase, whilst adding roman numerals. Finally, complete the harmonisation by adding the inner voices.

Numerals ______________________________

____

CHAPTER 10

HARMONIC ANALYSIS 2

These analysis extracts are linked to aural/visual observation where you will listen to the music while following the printed score. The emphasis here is on modulation but also includes decorative elements with which you are familiar. The extracts are taken from Baroque, Classical and early Romantic literature. While some extracts are from the beginning of a piece or movement, others are not. For the sake of simplicity in bar numbering, all extracts will be taken as beginning with bar 1.

You may listen to each audio extract as often as you wish.

Exercise 10.1 Audio 10.1

Listen as you study these opening bars from Bach's Goldberg Variations BWV 988 Var.18. Then answer the questions that follow.

(i) Name the key to which the music modulates in bars 3 and 4. ____________

(ii) Draw an asterisk below a chord that acts as a pivot chord.

(iii) What is the function of the circled notes in bars 2 and 4? ________________

(iv) Circle an auxiliary note.

Exercise 10.2 Audio 10.2

The following extract is the opening of a Scherzo from Petits Morceaux No. 12 by Bertini. Listen while you study the score to answer the questions in relation to it.

(i) Name the key in which the extract ends. ______________

(ii) What is the relationship between this key and the tonic key? ________________

(iii) Name the type of cadence confirming the new key in bars 15 and 16. ______________

(iv) In which bar is the new key first introduced? _________

(v) Identify and circle a chord of **V7d** in the tonic key.

(vi) Identify and circle an example of a suspension in the second half of the extract.

Exercise 10.3 Audio 10.3

Listen to and study the extract below from Schubert's Waltz Op. 127 No. 17. Then answer the questions that follow.

(i) Name the tonic key. ________________

(ii) Name the modulation that is confirmed at the cadence in bar 8. ____________

(iii) The modulation is first introduced in bar 6; is it approached by a pivot chord or a transition? ____________

(iv) Circle an example of a suspension in the last few bars of the extract.

Exercise 10.4 Audio 10.4

Below are the first two phrases of the chorale 'O Haupt voll Blut und Wunden' from Saint Matthew's Passion BWV 244 No.1. by J.S. Bach. Fill in the blanks in the sentences that follow to outline the keys, cadences and decoration.

The chorale begins in the key of ____________ which is confirmed by a ____________ cadence at the end of the first phrase. Phrase 2 is in the key of ___________. The new key is introduced by means of a ____________ (pivot/transition). Phrase 2 ends with a ____________ cadence. The quaver movement in the alto part on the last beat of bar 1 functions as a ____________. Passing notes are heard in the bass line of bar ____.

Exercise 10.5 Audio 10.5

The extract below is from Mendelssohn's Song without Words Op. 53 No. 5. Study the score while you listen, then answer the questions that follow.

(i) Name the key of bars 1 – 6 (beat 2). __________

(ii) Add roman numerals below the bass in bar 1.

(iii) Name the key in which the extract ends. __________

(iv) What type of cadence confirms the new key? ___________

(v) Draw an X above the chord that first introduces the new key.

(vi) Draw an asterisk above a chord that acts as a pivot for the modulation.

Exercise 10.6 Audio 10.6

Listen to the first two phrases of the chorale *'Hilf, Herr Jesu, lass gelingen'* printed below. Then answer the questions that follow.

(i) Name the key of the first phrase, bars 1 – 4. ___________

(ii) Name the type of cadence at the end of phrase 1. __________

(iii) Name the key of the second phrase, bars 5 – 8. ___________

(iv) Name the type of cadence that concludes phrase 2. __________

(v) What is the function of the tied G in the bass across bar 2 to 3? ___________

(vi) Circle two examples of a suspension and its resolution in the upper voices in phrase 1.

(vii) Does the music move through a pivot or transition to introduce the change of key? ____________

Exercise 10.7 Audio 10.7

Listen to this short extract from a Minuet in F by Mozart. Then answer the questions below.

(i) Bars 1 – 8 are based on the primary chords in F major; name the chords by adding roman numerals below the bass in bars 1 – 3.

(ii) Name the type of cadence reached at the end of the first phrase (bar 4) __________ and at the end of the second phrase (bar 8) _________

(iii) Draw a box around the notes of the dominant 7th chord in the second phrase.

(iv) What is the function of the circled notes in bar 4? _____________.

(v) From bar 9 the key changes; name the new key ____________

(vi) What type of cadence ends the extract? ___________

(vii) In bars 9 – 12 locate and circle a double suspension.

Exercise 10.8 Audio 10.8

The extract below is from *'Wiener Damen Lanola'* Op.67 No. 12 by Schubert. Answer the questions that follow.

(i) The opening 8 bars are based on 2 chords; using roman numerals name these chords. _____ and _____

(ii) From bar 9 the key changes to ____________.

(iii) Draw an asterisk on the music at the point where there is a return to the tonic key.

(iv) Is the return to the tonic made by means of a pivot or transition? ___________

Exercise 10.9 Audio 10.9

Listen to the first two phrases of a different setting of the chorale *'Hilf, Herr Jesu, lass gelingen'* printed below. Then fill in the blanks in the sentences that follow.

The chorale begins in the key of ________. A modulation is introduced in bar ___ to the key of ________. The new key reaches a ____________ cadence at the end of phrase 1. Phrase 2 returns to the key of _________. The chord on the first beat of bar 6 acts as a _________. Phrase 2 ends with a ___________ cadence. The alto voice decorates the harmony with a suspension in bar ___ beat ___. In bar ___ beat ___ the tenor voice has a suspension.

Exercise 10.10 Audio 10.10

The following extract is the first section of the main theme from Beethoven's Diabelli Variations. Listen carefully as you follow the score to complete the sentences and questions that follow.

(i) Bars 1 – 8 (beat 2) are in the tonic key and based on two chords, these are: ____ and ____

(ii) The music modulates in the area outlined by the red box. The key is ________

(iii) The chord on the 3rd beat of bar 8 is _________

(iv) Compare the areas outlined by the red and blue boxes, what do you notice?____________

(v) The area outlined by the green box changes key again to: _________

(vi) The chord on the 3rd beat of bar 12 is: _________

(vii) Name the key in which the extract ends. _________

(viii) Is this key arrived at through a pivot or transition? ____________

Exercise 10.11 Audio 10.11

Listen to the opening bars from the 4th movement of Beethoven's string quartet Op. 18, No. 2. Complete the questions that follow.

(i) Name the tonic key. ____________

(ii) The music first modulates in bars 7 and 8. The new key is ____________

(iii) What relationship does the key in bars 7 and 8 have to the tonic? ____________

(iv) Is this change of key approached by a pivot or transition? ____________

(v) Write roman numerals below the cello line in bar 7.

(vi) Bars 13 – 16 modulate again, this time to the key of __________; its relationship to the tonic key is ______________

CHAPTER 11

DIATONIC SEQUENCE and some SECONDARY 7th CHORDS

Modulating sequence has already been introduced in Chapter 9. Diatonic sequence refers to a pattern of progressions which do not modulate but belong within the one key. The cycle of 5ths provides a strong progression of chords on which to build a convincing sequence.

Audio 11.1

Listen to this extract from Caccini's *Ave Maria* based on familiar sequential patterns.

The cycle of 5^{ths} in major keys

The strongest chordal progression is **V – I**. All other chords with the same root relationship (i.e. falling a 5th) are also very strong and are the basis for creating a stylised sequence.

Beginning on the tonic chord in C major each of the following root chords fall a 5th.

Notice that very quickly the range becomes over extended.

Remember, the interval of a falling 5th is the same as a rising 4th, as it involves the same pitches. If we alternate these intervals a complete sequence beginning and ending on the tonic chord, all within range, is possible.

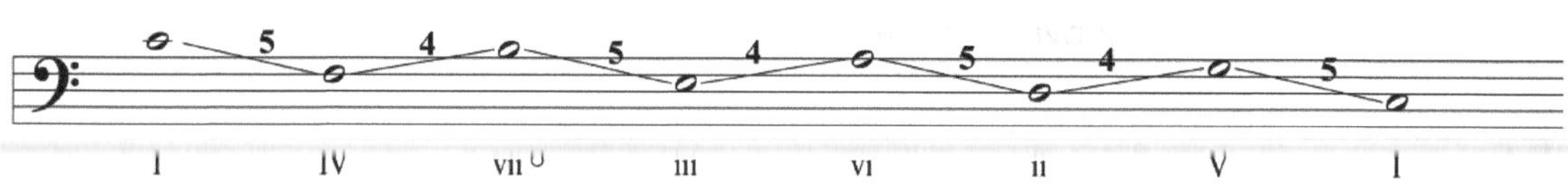

Because this is a diatonic sequence not all 4^{ths} and 5^{ths} are perfect intervals.

The less used chords of **iii** and **vii** occur naturally as the pattern unfolds.

Our previous example began with a falling 5th followed by a rising 4th. However, it is equally effective to begin with the interval of a rising 4th followed by a falling 5th.

The initial pattern of intervals chosen should normally be maintained throughout the sequence.

This example shows the completed chords in block formation.

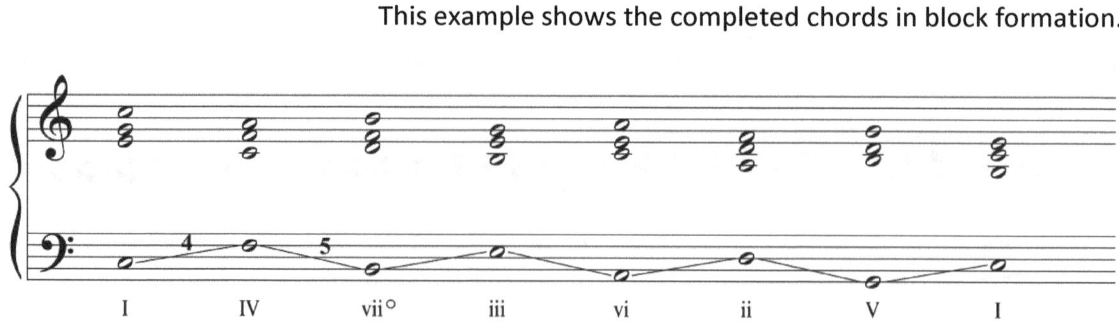

Audio 11.2

Listen to the previous sequence, noting the driving bass line which begins with the rising 4th.

The following pattern shows another presentation of the sequence.

Audio 11.3

Notice the falling 5th to begin the bass sequence while the treble uses a different layout.

Here is the sequence arranged for SATB.

- Notice how the melodic shaping is designed across a **pair of chords**. This is the model which is then applied sequentially to the remaining pairs of chords. So, while there are 8 chords in a complete sequence, globally there are 4 patterns.
- Two points worth noting regarding the leading note in bar 2: The leading note B in bar 2 does **not** rise to the tonic in bar 3 as it is governed by the sequential pattern which takes precedence in this instance.
  For the same reason the doubled leading note on the first beat in bar 2 is acceptable.

Audio 11.4

Notice how the quavers at the end of each bar (tenor) give forward impetus to the music.

Here is another arrangement in compound time.

On occasion, if the full sequence is used, it may be helpful to modify the melodic material towards the end, either to progress towards a cadence, or to prepare for a move in a new direction for what follows. This is the case in bars 3 and 4 of the example above.

Audio 11.5

Notice how the sequence is modified with more rhythmic activity towards the end of the phrase, pushing towards the cadence.

Exercise 11.1

Complete the following cycle of 5ths for SATB maintaining the opening model.

(a)

Numerals ____

(b)

Numerals ____

(c)

Numerals ____

(d)

Numerals ____

____

It is often the case that only a portion of the sequence is used which is demonstrated in the next example.

Audio 11.6

As you listen pick out the sequential area which uses progressions in a cycle of 5ths.

The cycle of 5ths can clearly be heard in bars 2 and 3 where the soprano and bass parts work sequentially. The pattern is maintained into the beginning of bar 4 and thereafter the movement is free.

In order to allow more flexibility in the bass part when using the cycle of 5ths the chords need not be limited to root positions. First inversions are helpful in shaping a more active bass line. Study examples a, b and c below.

(a)

In example (a) the first of each pair of chords begins on a first inversion.

> Remember, it is the **roots** of the chords that are a 5th apart, not necessarily the bass notes.

(b)

In example (b) above the second of each pair of chords moves from its first inversion to its root position.

(c)

In this final example (c) both chords of the pair make use of first inversions.

Audio 11.7

As you listen to the last 3 examples notice that the phrasing may not always follow the harmonic change. In example (b) the short quaver passing note at the end of each bar pushes the music forward across the bar line and is phrased with what follows.

Exercise 11.2

Complete each sequence for SATB based on the given models.

(a)

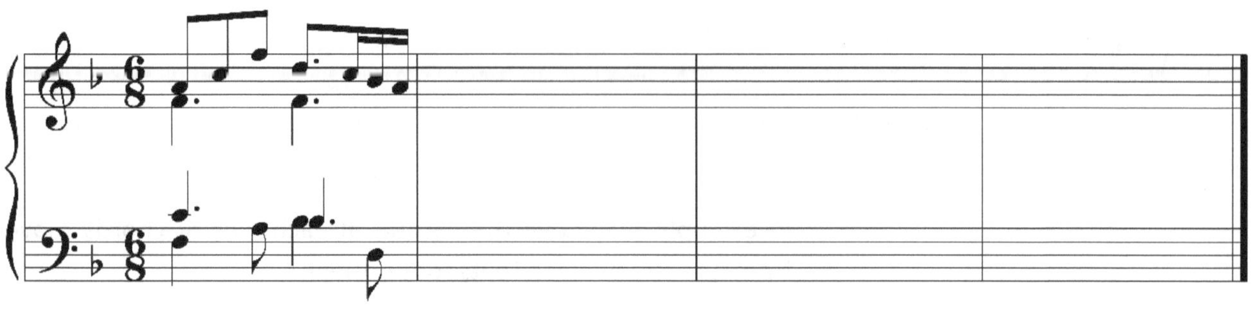

Numerals ____

(b)

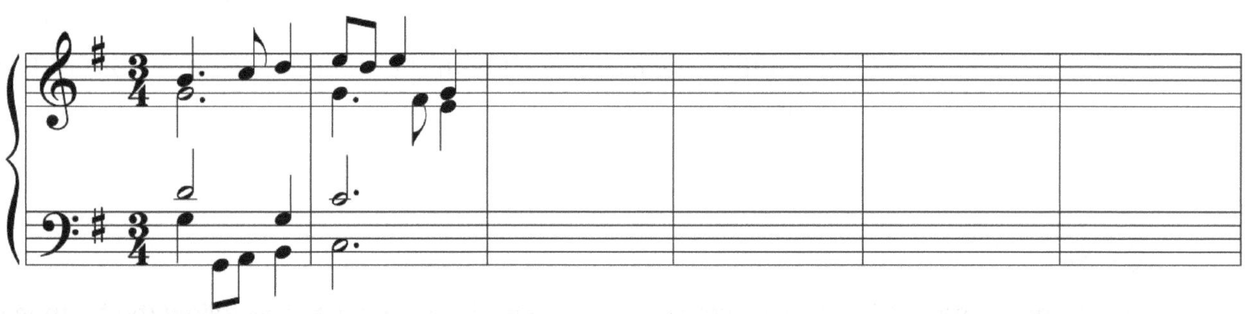

Numerals ____

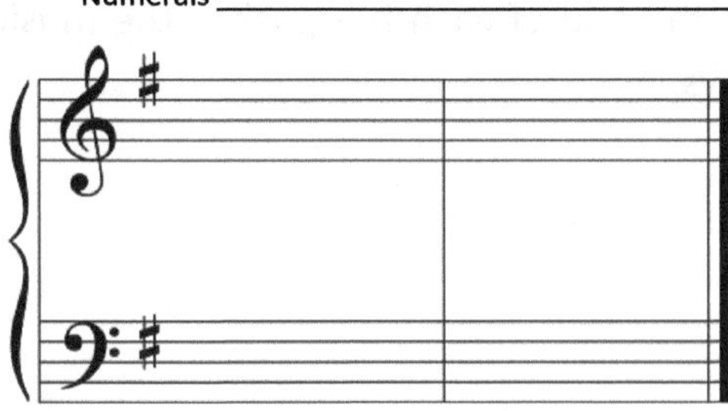

____

Exercise 11.3

(a) Complete the following cycle of 5^{ths} sequence by adding the bass line followed by the alto and tenor parts.

Numerals ____

(b) Complete the following cycle of 5^{ths} sequence by adding the soprano line followed by the alto and tenor parts.

Numerals ____

As has been seen already in an earlier example (Audio 11.6) the cycle of 5th sequence can be a useful feature at any point in a harmonisation. It may be complete or partial as appropriate. Listen and study the example below.

Audio 11.8

As you listen to Audio 11.8 notice the detail of phrasing. The upbeat at the beginning is also matched by the upbeat phrasing in the sequence area.

- In bars 2 and 3 effective use is made of a portion of the cycle of 5ths.
- In bar 4 the soprano continues in sequence. However, the rate of chordal progression is altered creating an acceleration which pushes towards the cadence.

Phrasing and chord change may not always syncronise

Exercise 11.4

Sing each of the following melodies noting any sequential shaping. Apply the cycle of 5[ths] progressions as may be appropriate. Work the complete bass line first followed by inner voices.

(a)

Numerals ______________________________

(b)

Numerals ______________________________

The cycle of 5ths in minor keys

The basic principals are the same when writing in the minor key. However, the quality of some chords is adjusted, notably those involving the 7th of the scale. Below is the cycle of 5ths in block formation using the flattened 7th. The flattened 7th is necessary in chords **VII** and **III**. However, the raised 7th is re-established in chord **V**.

Audio 11.9

Notice the prominent major sound as chords **VII** and **III** use the flattened 7th of the minor scale.

Study the following SATB example in A minor.

- In bar 2 the flattened 7th (G) is necessary to avoid ungainly intervals and preserve the natural flow of the sequence. Whereas in bar 4 the raised 7th is both necessary and expected in order to preserve the line whilst confirming the minor key.
- In bar 3 the use of the diminished chord **ii** in root position is governed by the sequential pattern and therefore is acceptable.

Audio 11.10

The quaver passing note at the end of each bar creates forward momentum; notice the phrasing.

Exercise 11.5

Continue each of the given opening models to create a complete cycle of 5^{ths} sequence. Modify the shaping at the end as appropriate.

(a)

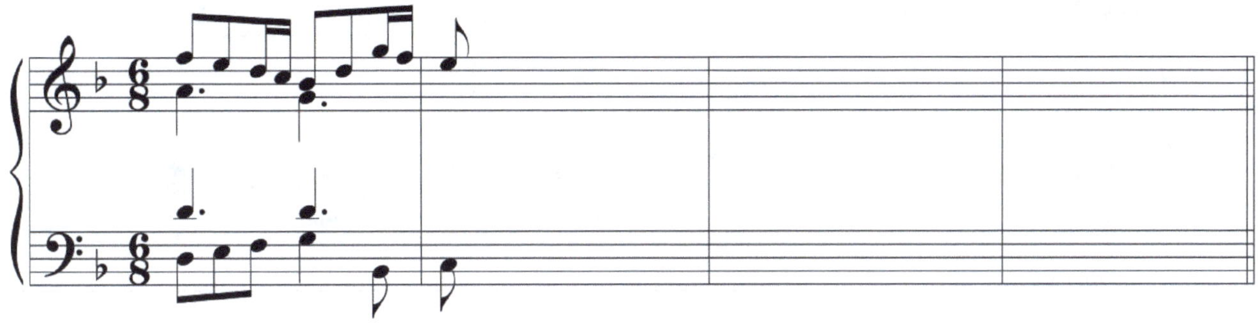

Numerals ____

(b)

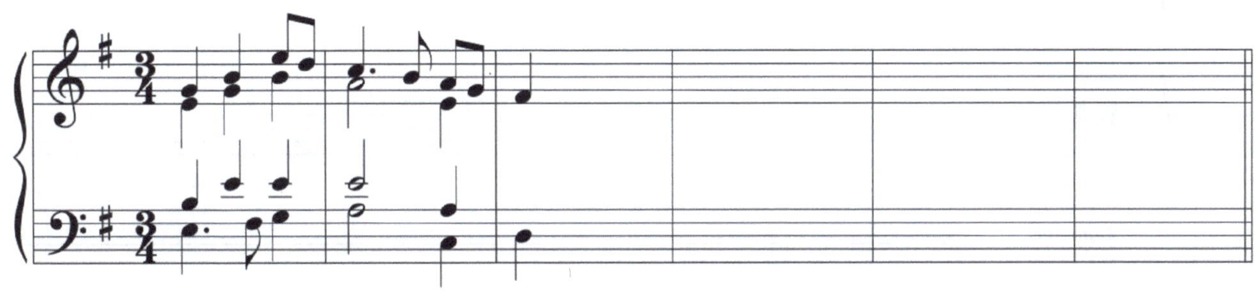

Numerals ____

Exercise 11.6

Complete each sequence for SATB. Phrase your completed work.

(a)

Numerals ______________________________

(b)

Numerals ______________________________

The following example in C minor makes use of a portion of the cycle of 5[ths] sequence.

Audio 11.11

Listen to the example above as you study the points that follow.

- Bars 2 and 3 have sequential treatment based on the cycle of 5[ths].
- Notice the strong implication of major tonality in bar 3*.

  (*The option to modulate into the key of E flat major presents itself here, however, for now we will bypass this opportunity and explore it at a later point).

- The final bars affirm the minor key.

Exercise 11.7

Sing each of the following melodies noting any sequential shaping. Apply the cycle of 5[ths] as appropriate. Work the complete bass line first followed by the inner voices.

(a)

Numerals ______________________________

____

(b)

Numerals ______________________________

____

Adding 7ths

You are already familiar with adding a 7th to the dominant chord. It is possible to add a 7th to other chords also. In doing so, a richer sound and a dissonance is created, which in turn needs resolution.

Audio 11.12

Listen to Audio 11.12 where you will hear again the Caccini extract from the beginning of the chapter. Some secondary chords have a 7th added – these are highlighted in blue. The same sequence of chords is used 3 times in these 24 bars, with some variation in the upper lines on each repeat.

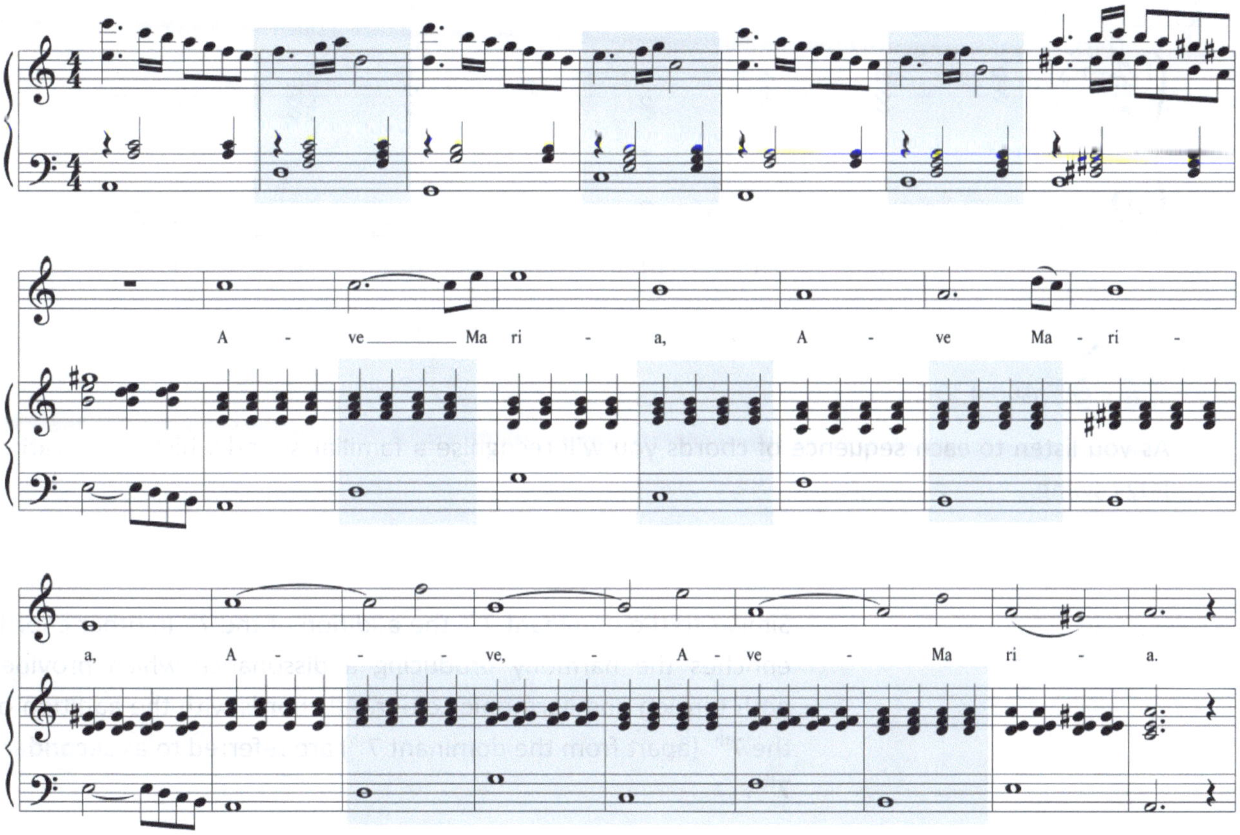

Let us rewrite the C major block chord sequence from earlier, to now include the 7th in each chord.

Similarly, here is the earlier C minor sequence with a 7th included in every chord.

Audio 11.13

As you listen to each sequence of chords you will recognise a familiar sound which has a rather jazzy swing.

Similar to the dominant 7th, the addition of the 7th in other chords enriches the harmony producing a dissonance which provides both tension and harmonic colour. All chords with the addition of the 7th (apart from the dominant 7th) are referred to as **secondary 7ths**.

- All 7ths will resolve downwards by step as the harmony changes.
- In the context of a sequence, the 7th may be added to each chord or alternate chord.
- It is normally the case that the 7th of any chord resolves down a step to the **3rd** of the following chord.

In both of the following examples the 7th is included and circled in every chord. The arrow shows the appropriate downward resolution in the next chord.

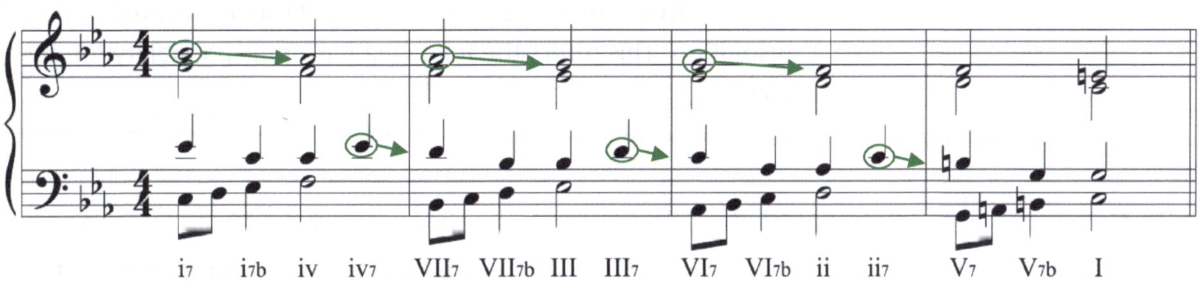

Audio 11.14

Listen carefully to each example as you study the score. Compare the first example in C major with the second in C minor.

> A melody note that falls a step offers the opportunity to be treated as a secondary 7th chord followed by its resolution

Sing or play this soprano line and then study some possibilities explored for harmonisation below.

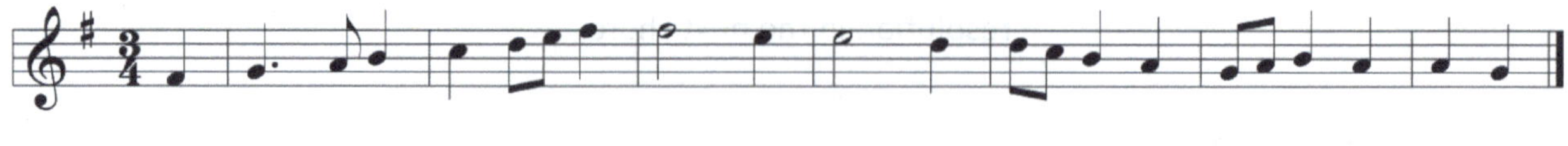

Here in bars 3 and 4 there is an easily identifyable sequence, featuring a repeated note followed by a downward step.

This profile would normally suggest the preparation and resolution of a suspension. However, a further option is to treat the repeated note as a secondary 7th and the downward step as its resolution. This offers the following harmonic possibility for bars 3 and 4.

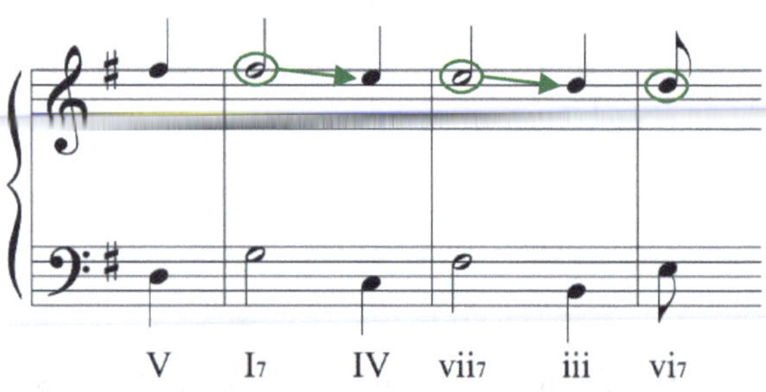

The fact that the F sharp leading note does **not** rise to the tonic indicates that it has a different function in this context. Notice that the 7th in each case resolves to the **3rd** of the next chord.

The next step is to complete the bass part.

The last 3 notes require cadential treatment. On this occasion the repeated note is treated as a suspension.

A sustained or repeated note that falls a step has the potential to be a secondary 7th chord followed by its resolution – but the context must be appropriate!

The final step is to add inner voices.

In bar 5 notice that the 7th in **vi7** on the first beat does not resolve directly in the soprano line, rather it is transferred to the tenor part on beat 2, which in turn resolves correctly in the following chord on beat 3.

Audio 11.15

In Audio 11.15 you will hear the four stages of the harmonisation beginning with the soprano alone, then the soprano and bass fragment followed by the complete soprano and bass parts and finally the full 4-part harmonisation.

Here is a summary of points to keep in mind as you work the exercises that follow.

Summary

- Look out for sequence in the given material and aim to compliment it in any of the added parts
- A sequence based on a cycle of 5ths may or may not include a 7th
- When a 7th is included it will resolve down a step to the **3rd** of the next chord
- The melodic profile of a repeated note followed by a downward step prompts the use of either a suspension or a secondary 7th harmony - choose whichever is appropriate in the context.

Exercise 11.8

Add roman numerals below the bass part. Complete the harmonisation by adding parts for alto and tenor voices.

(a)

Numerals ____________________

(b)

Numerals ____________________

Exercise 11.9

Using roman numerals analyse the chords as indicated by the figured bass. Craft a shapely soprano melody before completing the harmonisation with parts for alto and tenor voices.

(a)

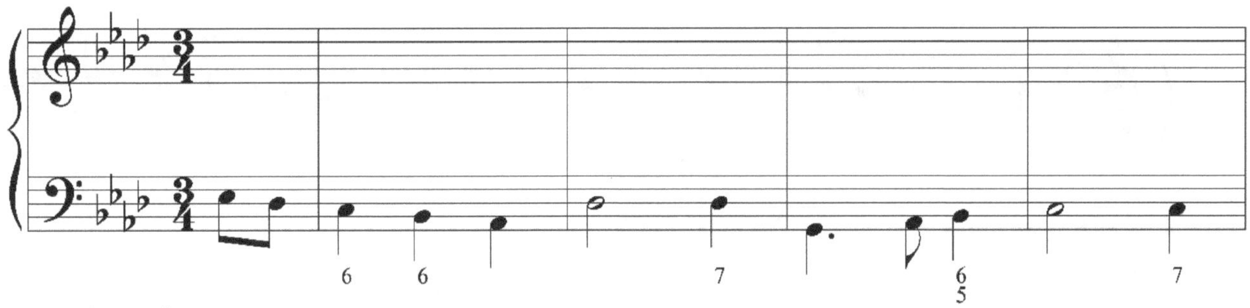

Numerals ______________________________

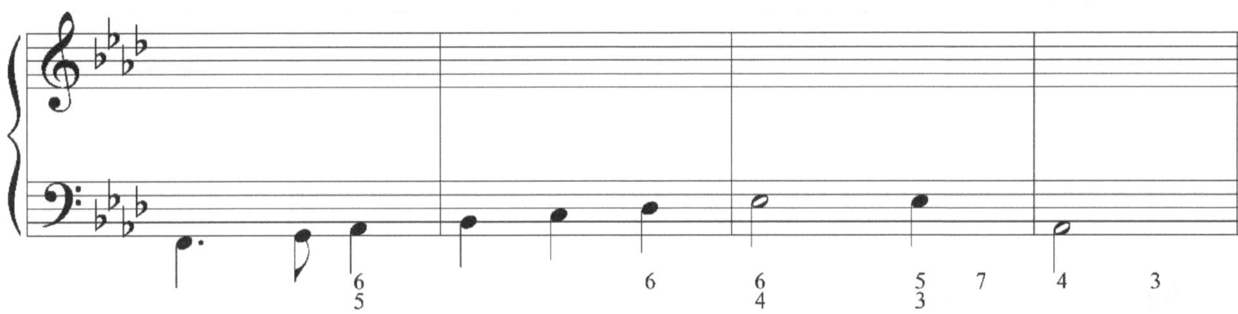

____

(b)

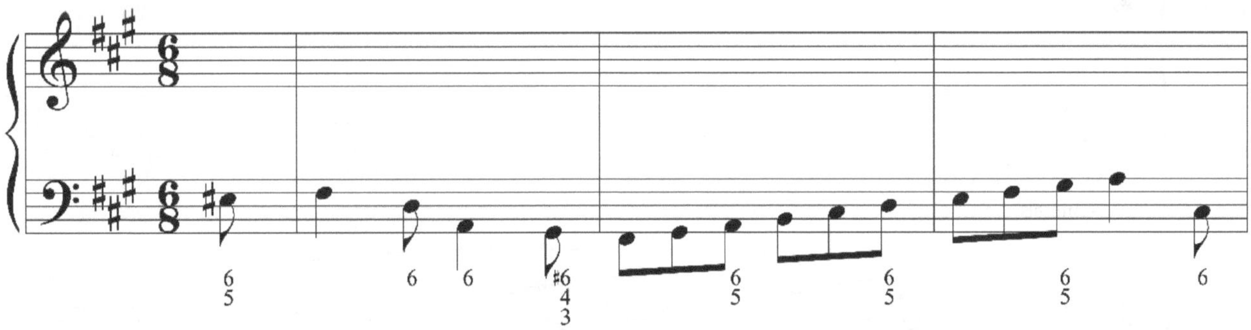

Numerals ______________________________

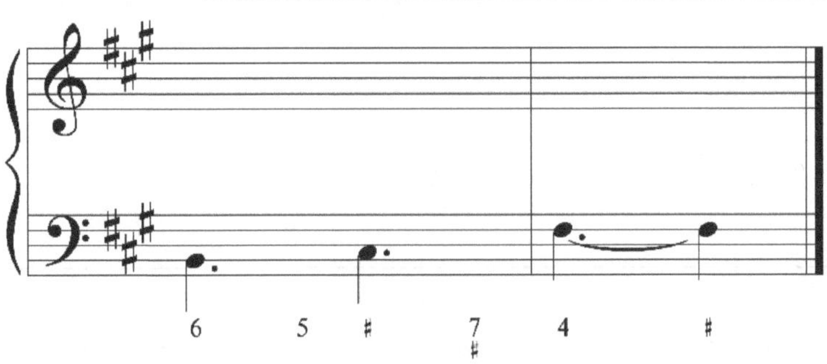

____

Exercise 11.10

Sing each soprano line noting any sequential shaping which could suggest the use of secondary 7[ths] in the harmony. Complete the bass line first followed by inner voices.

(a)

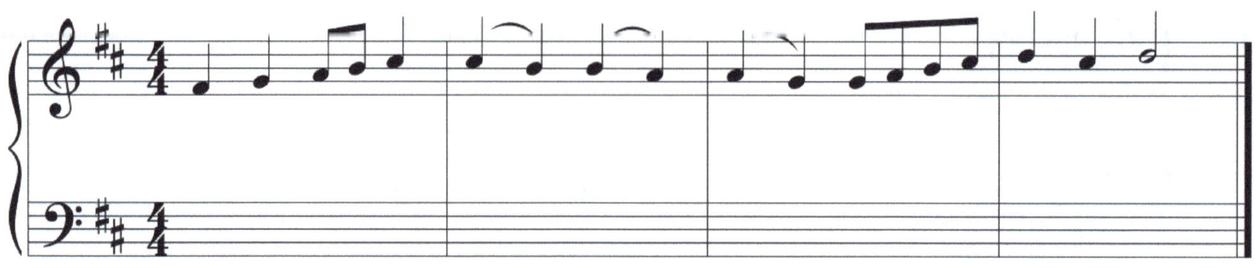

Numerals ________________________________

(b)

Numerals ________________________________

CHAPTER 12

MORE SECONDARY 7th CHORDS

You are already familiar with some 7th chords in the context of a cycle of 5^{ths} sequence. Adding 7^{ths} to chords is not limited to this use alone but may be used to enrich the harmony at any point.

Here are the chords in C major with the 7th added.

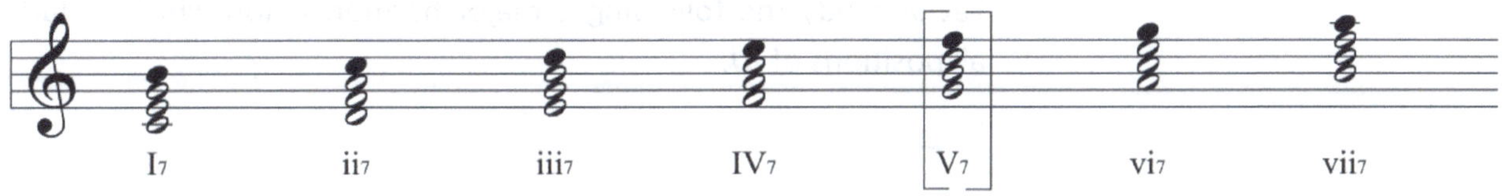

Audio 12.1

Listen to each secondary 7th chord as a broken chord.

Due to the fact that the 7th is a dissonance, it is common practice to approach it by step from a harmony note or by a repeated note. The 7th must always resolve downwards by step at the next chord change.

The most commonly used secondary 7th chord is **ii7**. The examples below show **ii7** in root position with the approach and resolution of the 7th highlighted.

Based on what we know of the dominant 7th, any chord with a 7th added potentially has four positions. Study the example below in relation to the chord of **ii7** with the figured bass included.

The 7th must always resolve down one step. The resolution is normally to the **3rd** of the next chord. Applying the resolution in this way will ensure a strong harmonic progression.

Let us study the following C major harmonisation which includes all positions of **ii7**.

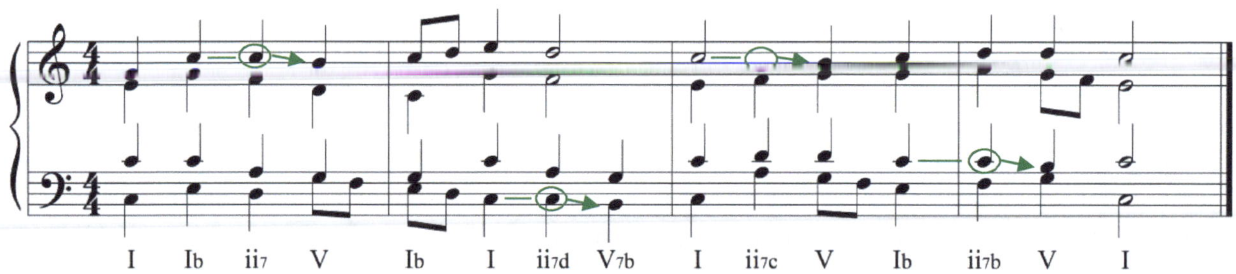

Audio 12.2

As you listen to the above example, note the different positions of **ii7** in each bar.

As a lead into using other 7th chords, it can be useful to remember that when the 7th resolves to the 3rd of the next harmony this will ensure a strong natural progression as shown below.

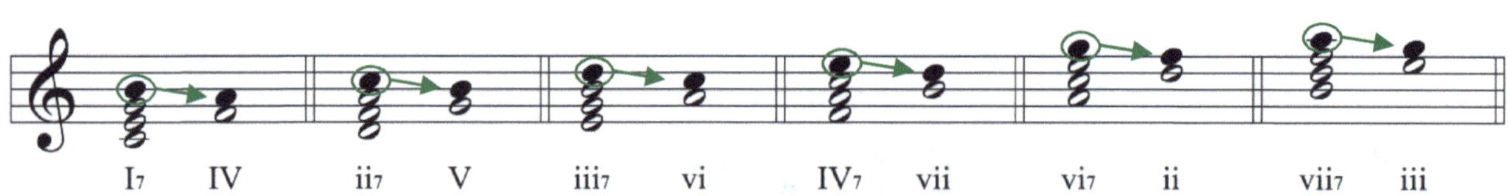

Some general points to remember . . .

- Never double the 7th
- Aim to include all four notes where possible
- The 5th may be omitted
- Each chord may be used in its four positions

The following harmonisation in G major makes use of a number of secondary 7th chords. The preparation, the 7th and the resolution are highlighted throughout.

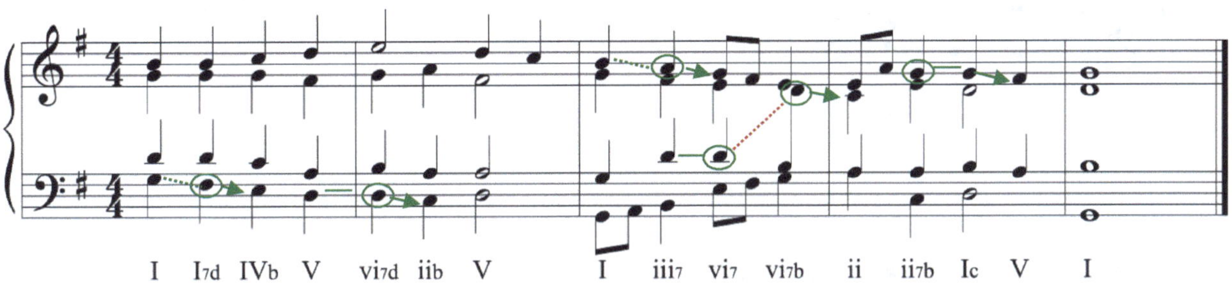

Bar 1: The 7th in **I7d** is approached by step from above and resolves downwards by step to **IVb**.

Bar 2: The 7th of **vi7d** is prepared by the repeated bass D in the previous bar and resolves down a step to **iib**.

Bar 3: The 7th of **iii7** is approached by step in the soprano part and resolves down a step to chord **vi**. However, the 7th is also included in **vi**, being prepared by a repeated note in the tenor part. Interestingly, the last beat of the bar moves to a first inversion of **vi** whilst transferring the 7th (D) from the tenor to the alto, resulting in **vi7b**. The 7th ultimately resolves in the next bar.

Bar 4: The 7th of **ii7b** is approached by step in the soprano part. Rather than resolving directly, it is threaded through the decorative **Ic** and ultimately resolves down a step in chord **V**.

Audio 12.3

Listen to the harmonisation above noting the rich quality created by the addition of the 7th in many chords.

Although it is quite common for the 7th of one chord to resolve down to the 3rd of the next chord, this is not the only possibility. Two factors must always be considered:

- The 7th (ultimately) must resolve downwards by step.
- The progression must be musically strong.

Some possibilities are outlined in the following examples.

The bass has a strong rising scale shape – ***s l t d***.

In this case the 7th of **vi7** resolves down by step to the 7th of **V7b**

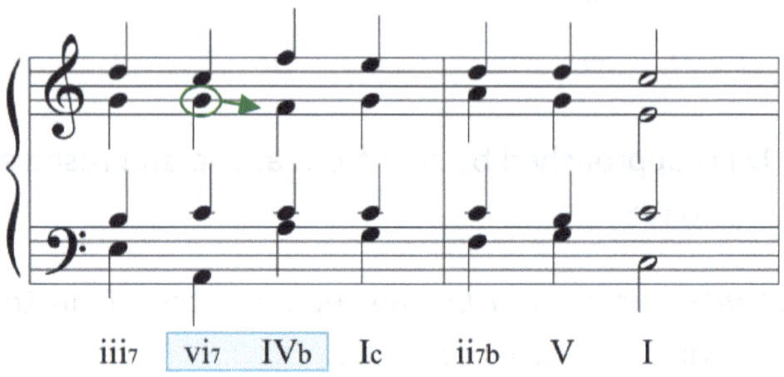

In this example the 7th of **vi7** resolves down a step to the root of **IVb**.

Audio 12.4

Listen to the above idiomatic progressions.

Exercise 12.1

Complete the harmonisation by adding parts for alto and tenor voices.

(a)

(b)

Exercise 12.2

Analyse the chords by including roman numerals below each bass line. Then write a shapely soprano melody followed by parts for alto and tenor.

(a)

(b)

Exercise 12.3

Harmonise each of the given soprano melodies. Look for opportunities to include some secondary 7th chords. Complete the bass line first followed by parts for alto and tenor voices.

(a)

(b)

Minor keys

Here are the chords with the 7^{ths} added in A minor.

At present, in minor keys the raised leading note is **not** part of chords **I7** , **III7** or **VII7**.

The following shows the 7th of each chord resolving to the 3rd of the next chord making a strong, natural progression in every case.

The following fragment in A minor is enriched by a variety of secondary 7th chords.

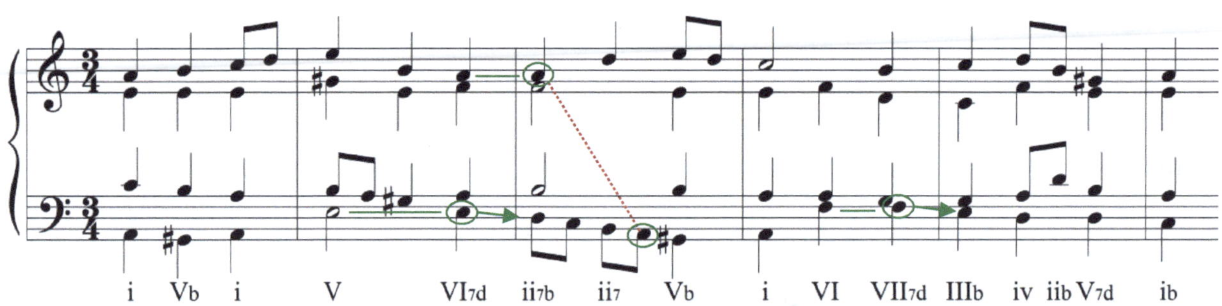

Bar 2: the 7th of **VI7d** is prepared by the repeated E bass note and resolves down a step in the next bar.

Bar 3: the 7th of **ii7b** is prepared by the repeated A in the soprano – it is then transferred to the bass following the move to the root position on beat 2 (essentially creating a brief **ii7d** position) and finally resolves down a step to **Vb** on beat 3.

Bar 4: the 7th of **VII7d** is prepared by the repeated F bass note and resolves down a step to **IIIb** in the next bar.

Audio 12.5

Listen to the above fragment noting in particular the effective change of chord on the repeated bass notes in bars 2 and 4.

Opportunity for modulation

Let us look again at the previous A minor example.

When the flattened 7th is used to form **VII7** (bar 4) we realise that it sounds exactly the same as the dominant 7th in the relative major key, thus providing a smooth path for modulation. By simply renaming the chord as a position of **V7** in C major, the change of key can easily be established by reshaping the harmony that follows to remain in C major to the end of the phrase as outlined below.

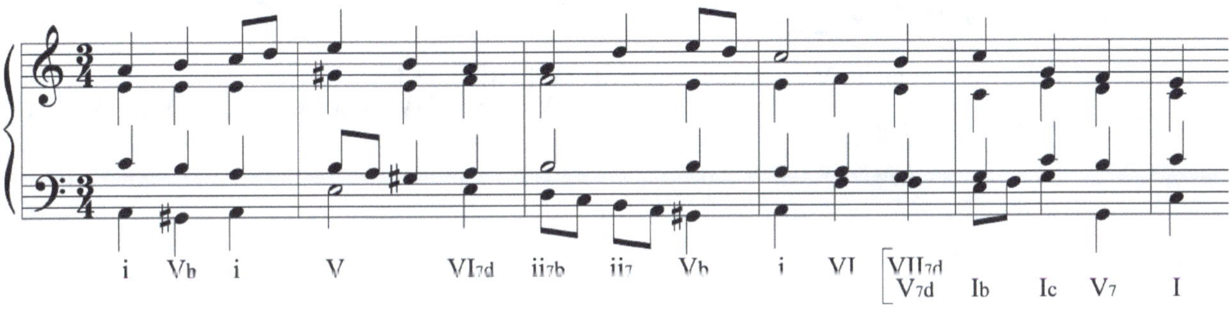

Audio 12.6

Comparing the end of this harmonisation to the previous one, you hear the final cadence of the fragment strongly affirms the key of C major.

Exercise 12.4

Each phrase begins in the minor key and modulates to the relative major. In each case complete the harmonisation by first writing a shapely soprano line followed by parts for the inner voices.

(a)

(b)

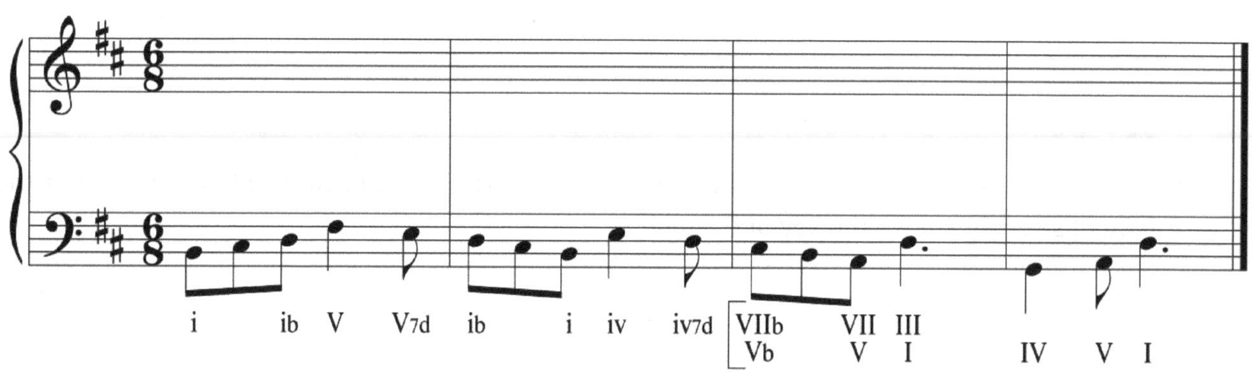

(c)

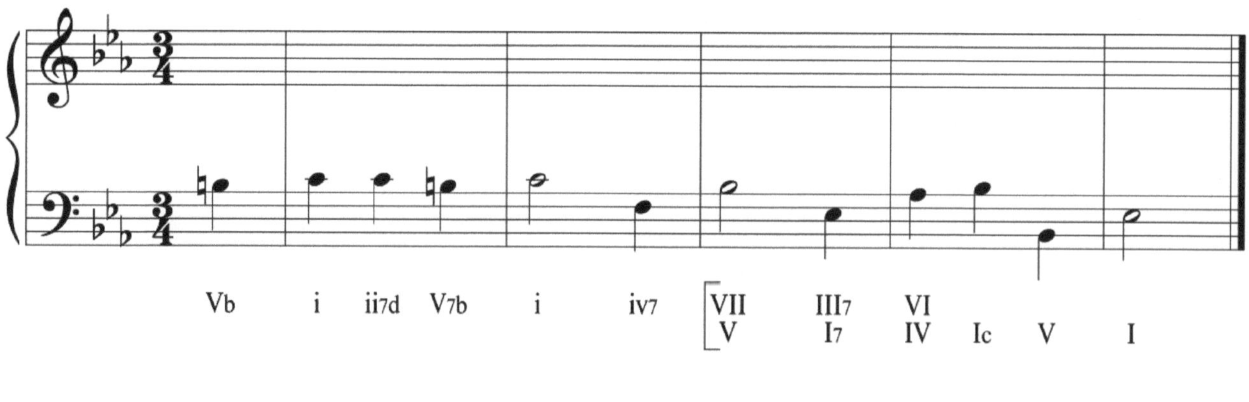

The diminished 7th chord

Up to this point in the minor key we have not used the raised 7th note when forming chords **I7**, **III7** and **VII7**.

However, a very distinctive chord with many uses is formed when the raised leading note is the root of **VII7** – thus producing a **diminished 7th** chord. This is a diatonic chord since it involves no accidental outside the key.

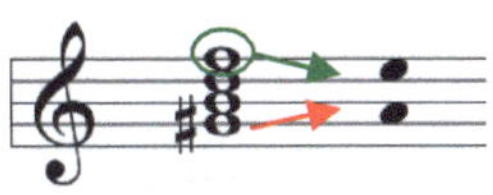

The most common use of **vii7** is to resolve to the tonic chord. The leading note rises a step as expected while the 7th of the chord falls a step thus resolving naturally into chord **i**.

This example shows the progression in A minor. Note the diminished 5th followed by the perfect 5th in soprano and alto parts is acceptable.

Study this harmonisation in A minor which includes the diminished 7th chord.

Bar 1: The diminished 7th **vii7** sits easily between the two positions of the tonic chord.

Bar 3: The diminished 7th in its first inversion **vii7b** has the 7th (F) prepared in the tenor part and resolves down by step to E in the following chord **ib**.

Audio 12.7

As you listen to the above example focus on the diminished 7th chords in bars 1 and 3.

Exercise 12.5

Complete each harmonisation by adding parts for alto and tenor voices.
In (b) add roman numerals below the given figured bass line.

(a)

(b)

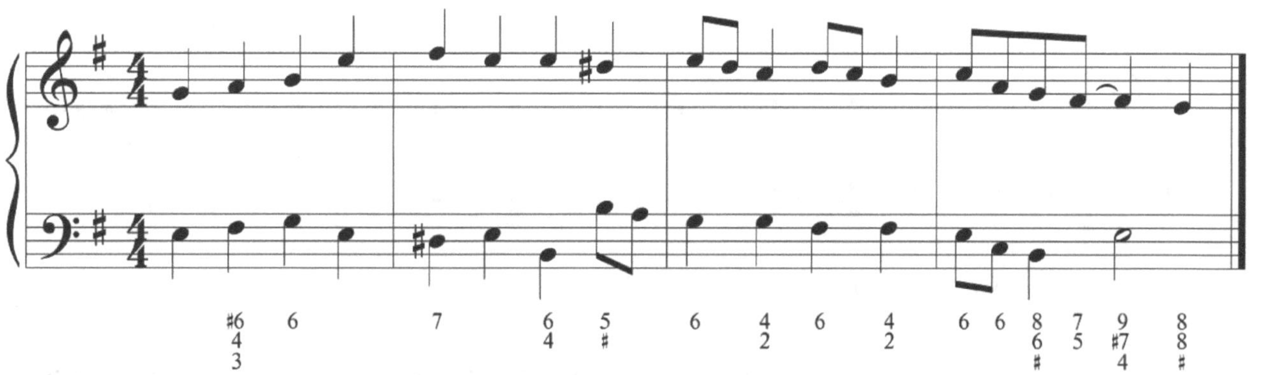

Exercise 12.6

Add roman numerals below each of the given figured bass lines. Then shape a melodic line for the soprano. Finally, complete the harmonisation by adding parts for alto and tenor voices.

(a)

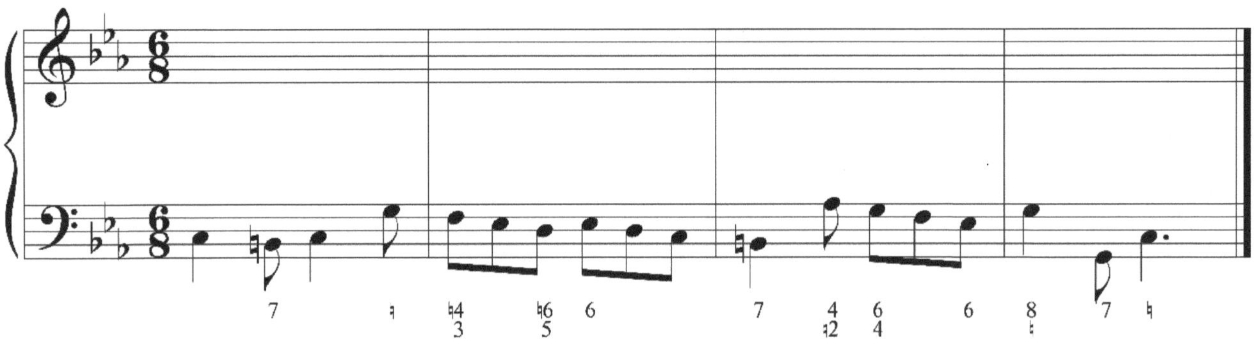

(b)

CHAPTER 13

CHROMATICISM - an introduction
Secondary dominant/Local dominant chords

Chromatic chords contain accidentals that are not part of the key signature or the melodic minor scale. These chromatic chords create harmonic colour without changing key.

Audio 13.1

Listen to the following two short extracts from piano sonatas by Mozart. The passages demonstrate some attractive harmonic colouring while remaining in the tonic key. The secondary dominant chords are highlighted on the score.

Mozart, Sonata in D major, K 311, 3rd mvt.

Mozart, Sonata in F major, K 533, 3rd mvt.

Any major or minor chord may be enhanced by **preceding** the chord with its own dominant/dominant 7th chord.

Finding the secondary dominant (local dominant)

- The **root** of the secondary dominant will always be a perfect 5th above (4th below) the chord to which it is attached.
- The chord will always be a **major** triad with a minor 7th added.
- The necessary **accidental(s)** create the colour in the harmony.

Here are the major and minor chords in C major and A minor. Each is preceded by its secondary dominant chord. The necessary resolutions are shown by the arrows.

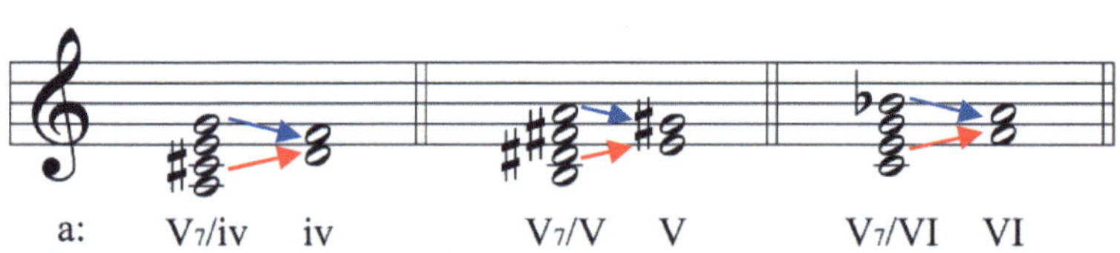

Each pair of chords can be seen to form a mini **V7 – I** progression without challenging the overall tonality.

Note the format of the roman numeral labelling, e.g., **V7/ii** reads as **V7** of **ii**, emphasising the fact that chord **ii** retains its function in the tonic key and no modulation has occurred.

The secondary dominant is termed a chromatic chord since an accidental or accidentals outside the key will always be present.

V7/V

This is the most commonly used secondary dominant often included to give a colourful approach to a cadence.

Here is a familiar cadential progression using **ii7 - V - I** with the typical soprano shaping of ***r - r - d***.

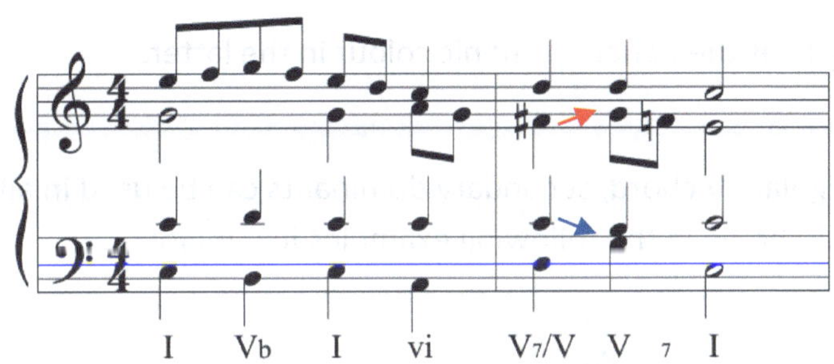

The introduction of the secondary dominant **V7/V** enriches the cadential effect while retaining the typical ***r - r - d*** soprano line.

It is generally best to approach the chromatic note(s) in a smooth way. The arrows indicate the necessary resolution of the secondary dominant chord.

Audio 13.2

Listen and compare both examples above. Note the increased harmonic colour when the secondary dominant chord is included.

Here is a conventional approach to the imperfect cadence.

The example is rewritten below to show the cadence enhanced by the secondary dominant chord. In this case the secondary dominant is not followed directly by chord **V** but travels through the decorative **Ic** before reaching chord **V**.

Audio 13.3

Comparing both previous examples you will hear the richer harmonic colour in the latter.

Inversions

As with a regular **V7** chord, secondary dominants can be used in all inversions as shown in the following examples in C major.

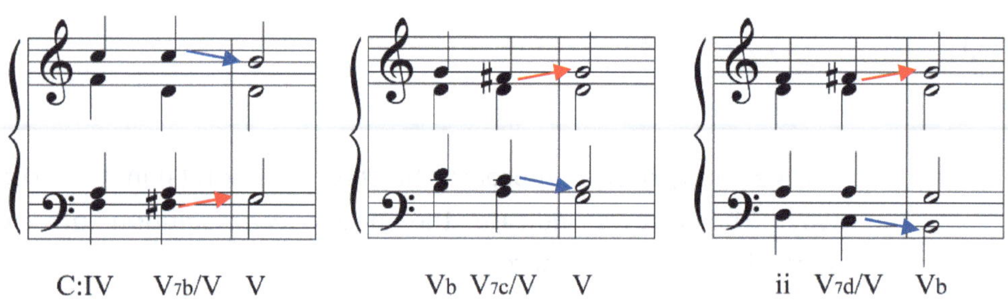

Audio 13.4

As you listen to the 3 examples above, notice the smooth approach to the chromatic element and its necessary resolution.

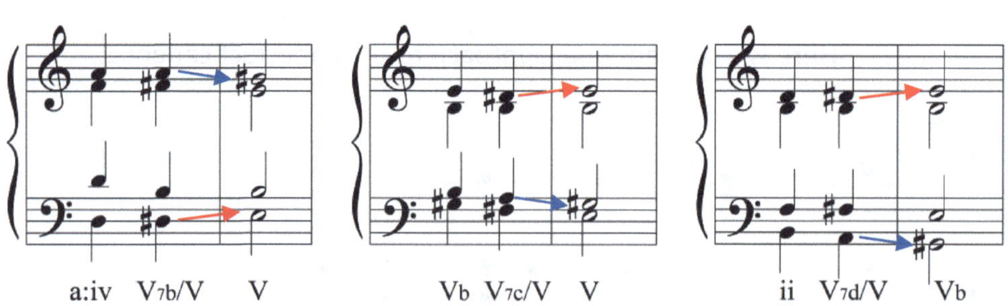

Audio 13.5

Now listen to the examples above in A minor.

Exercise 13.1

Analyse the harmony by adding roman numerals. Complete parts for alto and tenor voices.

(a)

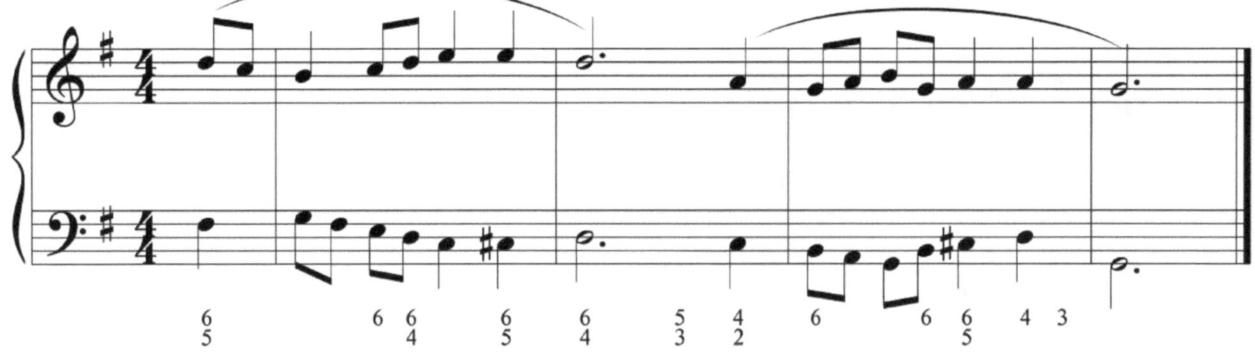

(b)

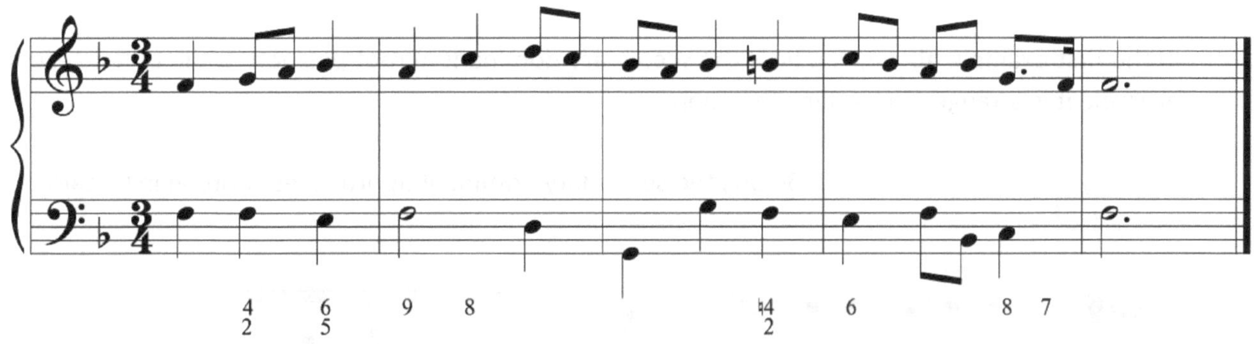

(c)

V7/ii

The following examples show secondary dominant chords effectively approaching chord **II** in C major.

Audio 13.6

In the first example above, you hear the secondary dominant in root position, while in the second example it is arranged in its third inversion.

V7/vi

Below, the secondary dominant approaches chord **vi** in C major.

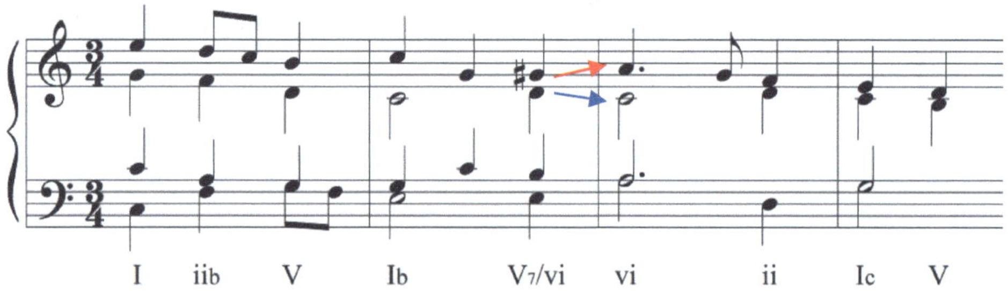

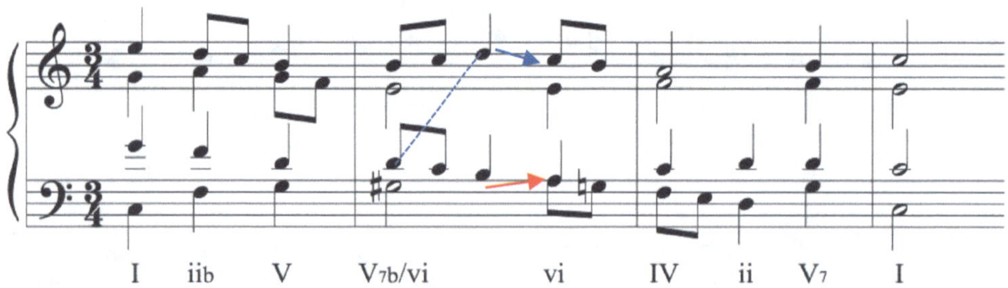

Audio 13.7

In these phrases the chromatic element is heard in soprano and bass parts respectively.

Let us look at an example of the secondary dominant approaching chord **VI** in the minor key. Note that by contrast to the major key, **V7/VI** in the minor key requires a flattened accidental in its structure.

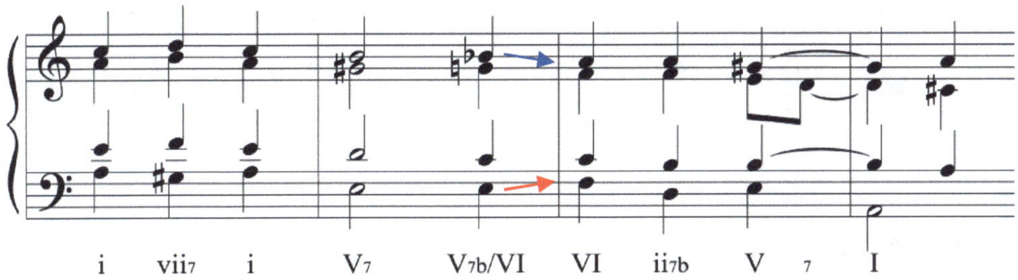

Audio 13.8

As you listen to this phrase in A minor, notice the very smooth part movement in bar 2 as the secondary dominant re-harmonises the repeated bass note.

Exercise 13.2

Add roman numerals to interpret each figured bass. The progressions **V7/ii** and **V7/VI** are included. Complete the harmonisations by adding parts for alto and tenor voices.

(a)

(b)

(c)

V7/IV

Study the next examples in which the secondary dominant approaches chord **IV**. The first two fragments are in C major; note the necessary flattened accidental here.

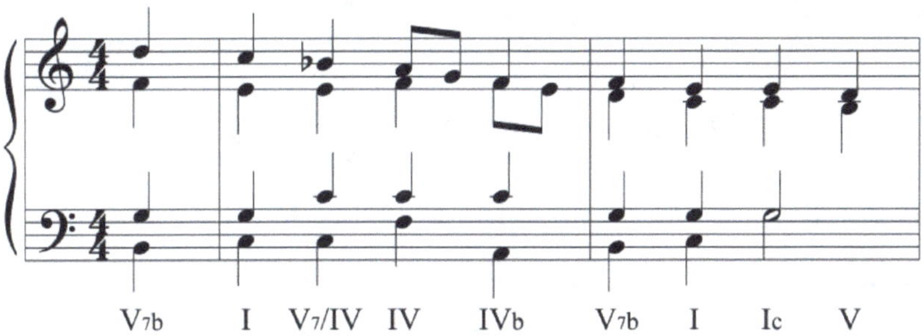

Audio 13.9

As you hear the 2 examples above, listen particularly for the voice that introduces the flattened accidental.

The following example is in the key of A minor.

Audio 13.10

Listen to the secondary dominant chord as it colours bar 2, while the final cadence is decorated with a 4-3 suspension which resolves to a Tierce de Picardie chord.

V7/iii

The next 2 examples show the secondary dominant approaching chord **iii** in C major.

(a)

(b)

Audio 13.11

In example (b) the secondary dominant chord in bar 2 is extended by using different inversions before reaching its resolution in chord **iii**.

Audio 13.12

Listen to this short extract while studying the score. The key in this area is A major but the harmony is extensively coloured with the use of secondary dominant chords.

Mozart, Sonata in D major, K 311, 3rd mvt.

Exercise 13.3

The following exercises include a variety of secondary dominant chords. Add roman numerals to label the progressions as indicated by the figured bass. Add parts for alto and tenor voices to complete each 4-part harmonisation.

(a)

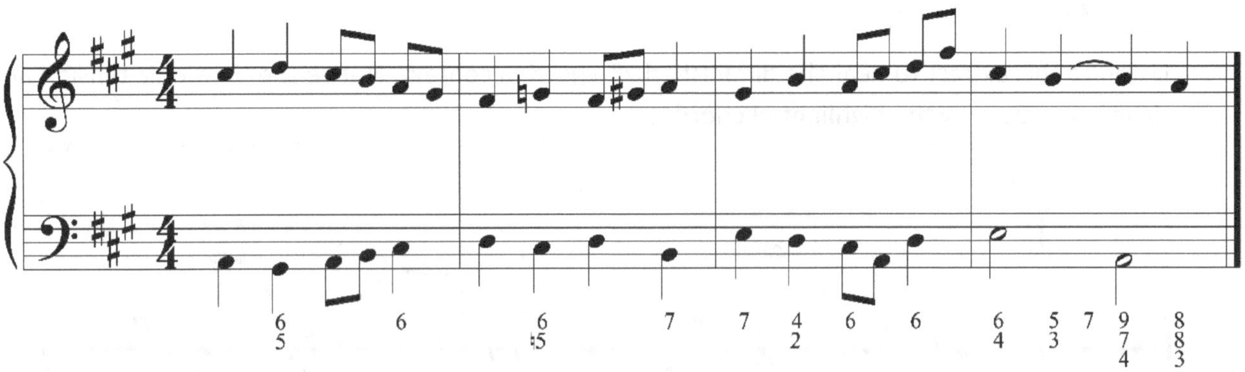

(b)

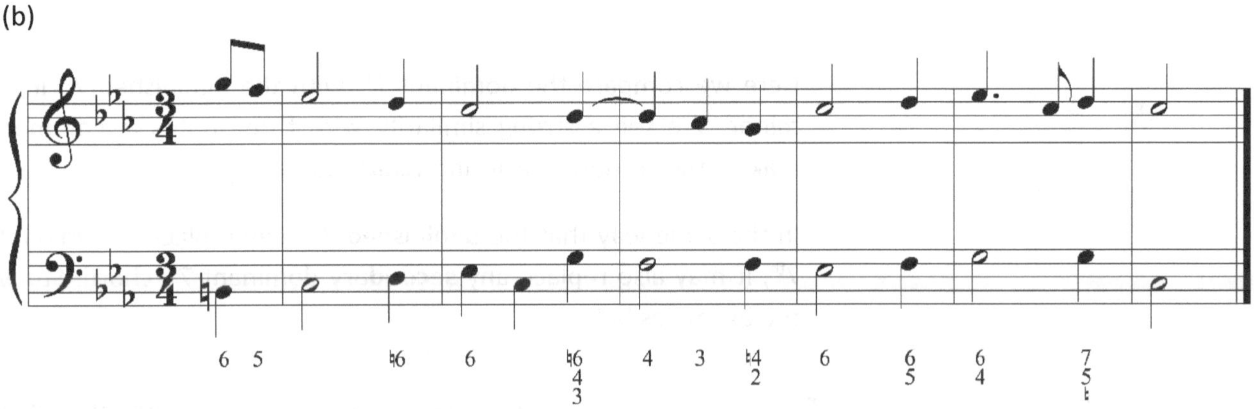

(c)

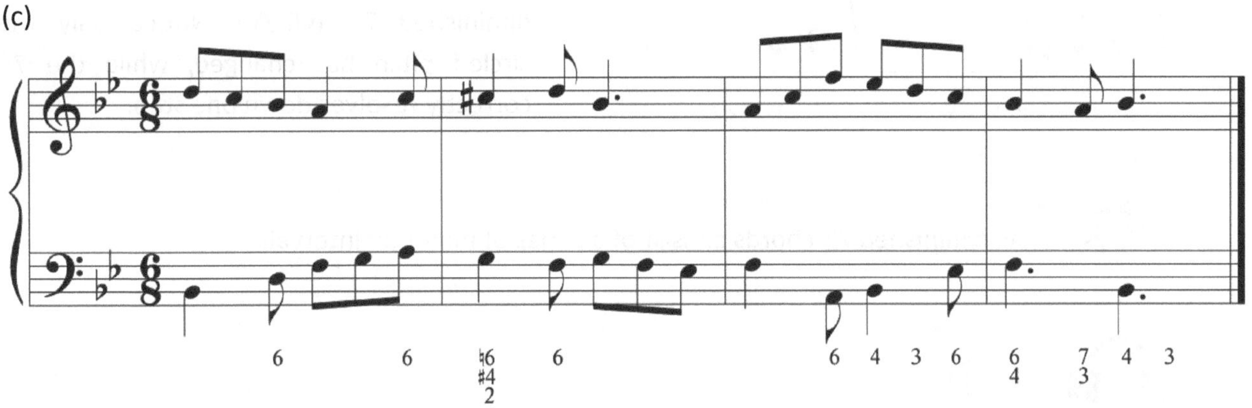

More on the diminished 7th

The diminished 7th chord was briefly introduced at the end of the previous chapter as an effective diatonic progression between two statements of the tonic chord in root position in minor keys.

Audio 13.13

Listen to this extract to hear the diminished 7th chord in context. Notice the harmonic tension and richness created by the highlighted chords.

Mozart, Sonata in C minor, K 457, 1st mvt.

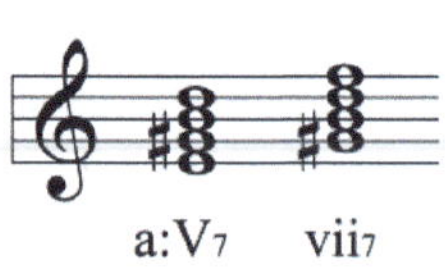

Here we compare the dominant 7th with the diminished 7th in A minor. We see a strong similarity with three notes in common making these chords easily interchangeable.

In the same way that the diminished 7th may replace a dominant 7th, it may also replace any **secondary** dominant 7th chord. Study the examples below.

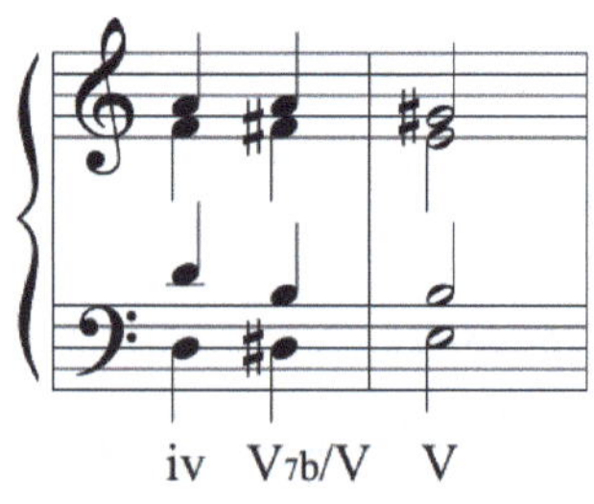

We are already familiar with the first example using a secondary dominant. The second example replaces **V7b/V** with the diminished 7th (**vii7/V**). Notice only the circled pitch has changed, while the 7th correctly resolves down one step.

All diminished 7th chords consist of a series of minor 3rd intervals

Audio 13.14

Compare **V7b/V** with the diminished 7th **vii7/V** in the previous examples in A minor.

IV V7b/V V

IV vii7/V V

Taking an earlier C major example, we can replace **V7b/V** with **vii7/V**. Notice the necessary E flat accidental to achieve the correct structure of the diminished 7th chord.

Audio 13.15

Compare the progressions above in C major.

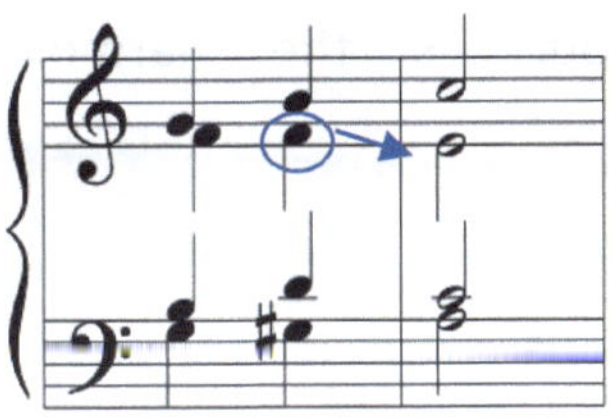

C:V7 vii7/vi vi

C:I vii7/ii ii

Similarly, the diminished 7th may replace **any** secondary dominant chord as seen in these examples.

Audio 13.16

Listen to the fragments above demonstrating the diminished 7th chord as an embellishment of **vi** and **ii**.

The **diminished 7th** may be used as an alternative to any **regular dominant 7th** or any **secondary dominant 7th** chord

Let us look again at this example which occurred earlier in the chapter (page 202). Bar 2 offers potential to introduce the diminished 7th - two possibilities are shown below.

Introducing the diminished 7th on the quaver intensifies the colour as the harmony progresses.

Alternatively, the diminished 7th may be used in an inversion at the beginning of the bar and re-arranged on the quaver.

It is advisable to use dominant harmony followed by diminished and not the reverse

Audio 13.17

Listen to the complete phrase which uses the first alternative in bar 2.

Audio 13.18

Listen once more to the passage to hear the second alternative in bar 2.

A secondary dominant (with a 7th) is essentially a major triad with a minor 7th added

A diminished 7th is a series of minor 3rds

A secondary dominant elevates the sound of the chord that follows it, whereas the diminished 7th further intensifies the chord that follows it.

Exercise 13.4

Complete the alto and tenor parts in the following passages.

(a)

(b)

(c)

Exercise 13.5

Analyse the progressions in these figured bass passages by adding the roman numerals below the stave. Complete the harmony by writing parts for alto and tenor voices.

(a)

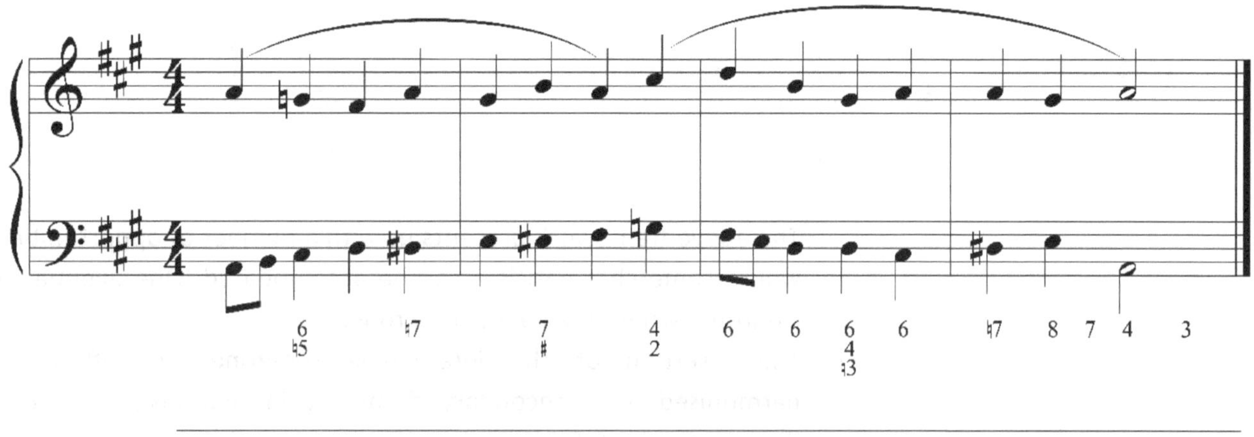

(b)

Let us take a phrase based on simple progressions without decoration and explore ways of enhancing the harmony.

(a)

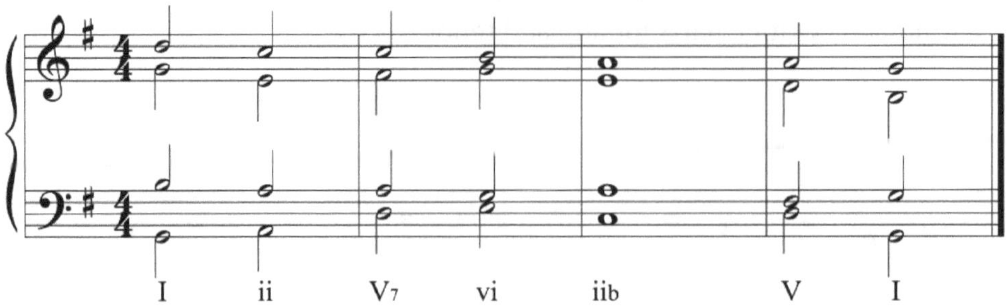

The above framework presents us with a number of opportunities where some chromaticism can be accomodated. One avenue to explore is where the bass rises a tone.

The insertion of the intervening semitone can often be harmonised as a secondary dominant in first inversion **or** a diminished 7th of the following chord.

This bass line offers 3 instances of rising tones.

By inserting the intervening semitone both secondary dominant and diminished 7th chords are possible as shown below.

(b)

This version harmonises the 3 potential points with secondary dominant chords.

(c)

A final harmonisation creates a more intensified version using a combination of secondary 7th and diminished 7th chords.

(d)

Bar 1, beat 2: The diminished 7th chord must have a series of minor 3rds hence the F natural in the alto line.

Bar 2, beat 2 uses the diminished 7th chord. Further interest is achieved on beat 4 by modifying the bass passing note D to become part of **vi7d**.

Bar 3 uses both the secondary dominant (beat 3) followed by the diminished 7th (beat 4) building the intensity towards the cadence.

Audio 13.19

Listen to the 4 stages (a, b, c, d) of the working which culminates in a rich harmonisation based around the original material.

This simple harmonic framework in the minor key adopts the same 4 stage approach.

(a)

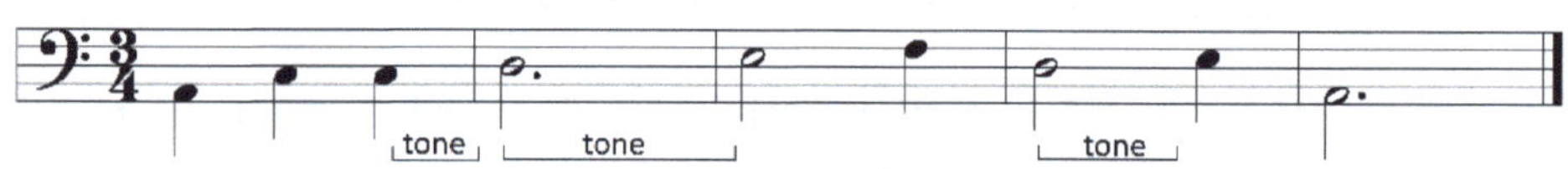

The 3 examples of a rising tone allow a chromatic semitone to be inserted with the possibility of using the secondary dominant and/or diminished 7th colouring.

(b)

In this version the 3 chromatic semitones are harmonised by secondary dominant chords resolving appropriately into the following chords.

(c)

The final version gives further intensity to the harmony.

(d)

Whilst the 3 chromatic semitones are now harmonised by the more dissonant diminished 7th some modification is needed in the part writing. The contour of the soprano line has changed from bar 2 onwards to accommodate the diminished 7ths and the necessary resolutions.

In bar 3 an extra chromatic chord is used to link chords **V** and **VI**; the bass, already a rising semitone, is reharmonised on beat 2 by using the secondary dominant (in first inversion) of chord **VI**. Here we see the movement from one dominant 7th directly to a different dominant 7th. The original leading note G sharp (alto beat 1) does not rise to the tonic but is re-routed into a new dominant 7th. The chromaticism is most effective when it moves by step. The secondary dominant resolves as expected.

Audio 13.20

Listen to the 4 stages (a, b, c, d) of the working which culminates in a rich harmonisation based around the original material.

Exercise 13.6a

Use the given simple SATB phrase as a basis for enhancing the harmony in the following stages:

(i) Rewite the bass line to include potential chromaticism in the form of rising semitones.

(ii) Using your new bass line complete the harmony using secondary dominant chords.

(iii) Finally, re-harmonise the new bass line using diminished 7th chords or a mixture of secondary dominant and diminished 7th harmony.

Feel free to adjust the original upper voices at any point where necessary to accommodate your enhanced reworkings. Include roman numerals at each stage.

(i)

(ii)

(iii)

Exercise 13.6b

Work through the same stages as laid out in exercise 6a.

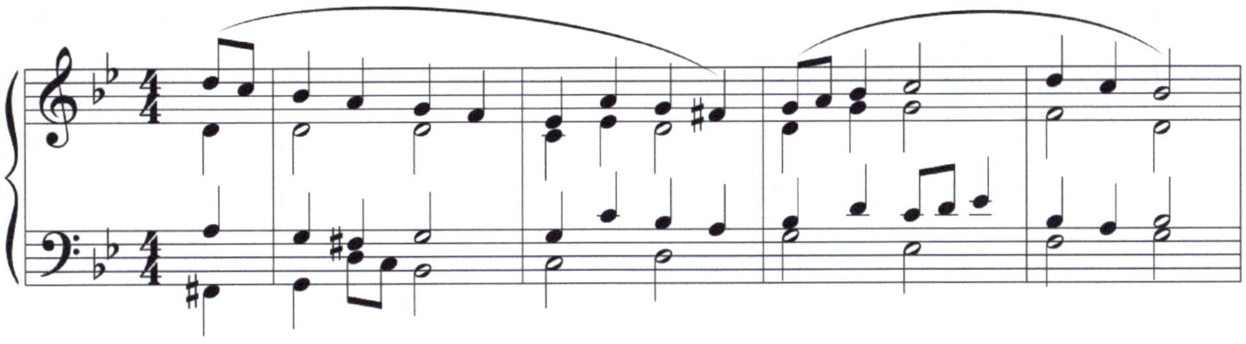

(i)

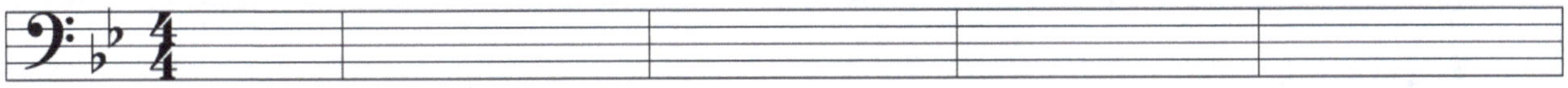

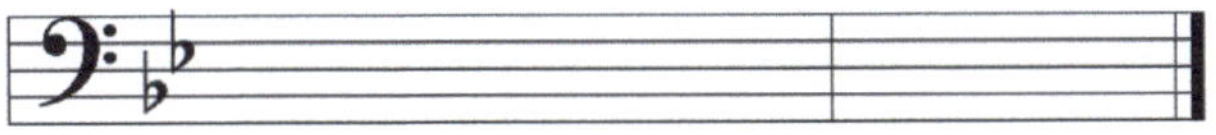

(ii)

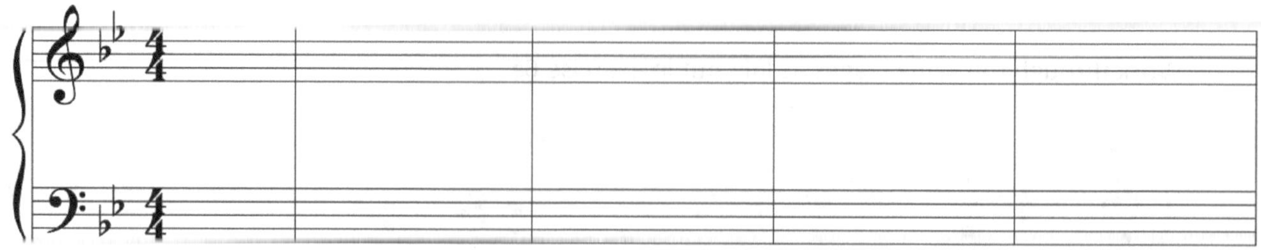

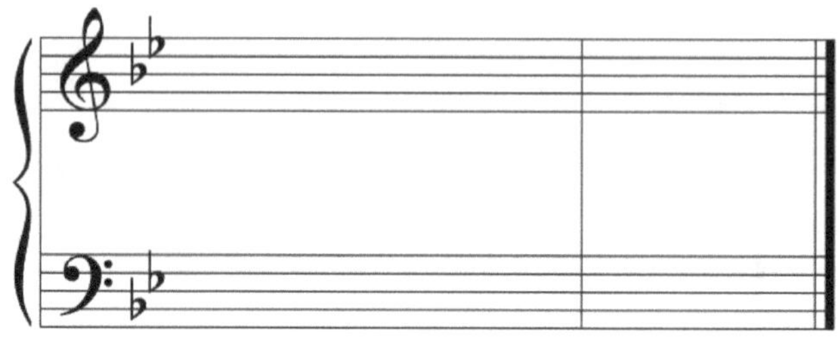

(iii)

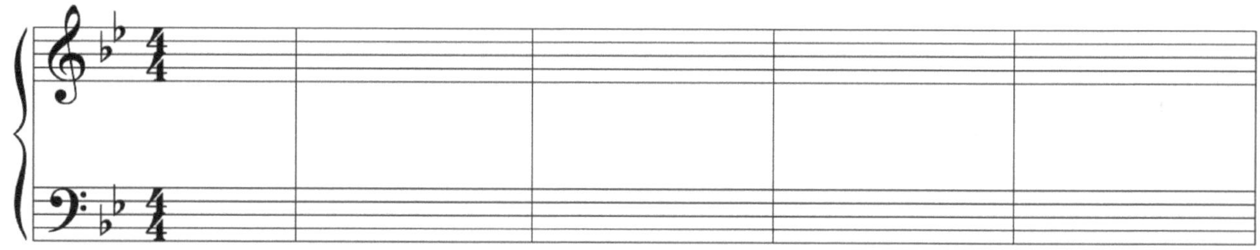

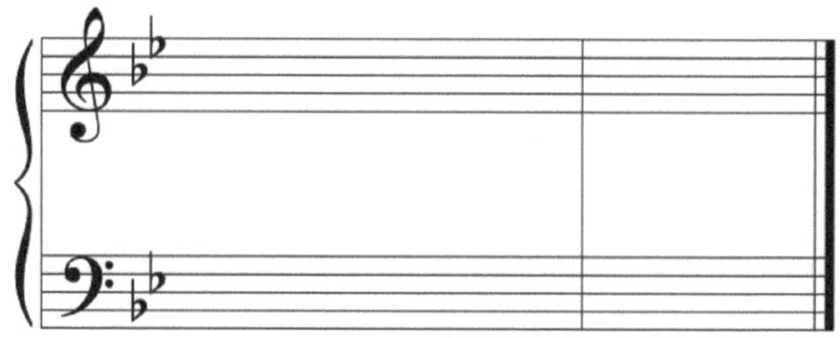

Let us study this F major bass line and work through some harmonic possibilities.

Audio 13.21

Listen first to the bass line alone, then the 4-part harmonisation while studying the commentary below.

Bar 1 uses **vii7** to colour the tonic harmony.

Bar 2 mimics the profile of bar 1 with the use of **vii7/V** while the suspension at the end of the bar pushes the line on.

Bar 3 (beats 1-3): The new colour can in fact be analysed in either of these 2 ways:

Secondary dominant in F major **or** a brief modulation to g minor.

Bar 4: The cadence establishes a modulation to the dominant key of C major; with this in mind the last beat in bar 3 is logically interpreted as chord **V** in C major.

Bars 5 and 6: The harmonic pace increases through the rising sequence as the diminished 7th chords add colour and intensity.

Bar 7: The descending profile and simple harmony relaxes the tension whilst the splash of colour on beat 4 enriches the final cadence.

Exercise 13.7

Study the given bass lines considering appropriate use of secondary dominant/diminished 7th chords. Add roman numerals to show your choice of chording. Shape the soprano line before completing inner voices.

(a)

(b)

(c)

CHAPTER 14

CHROMATIC MELODIC DECORATION
Passing notes. Auxiliary notes. Appoggiaturas.

In the previous chapters we have focused on chromatic chords to enrich the harmony; we will now turn our attention to chromatic decoration in the melodic lines which also creates additional colour and interest.

Listen to the following audio extracts while studying the scores. The circled notes pinpoint various decorative features.

Audio 14.1

The circled note in bar 1 of this extract is a chromatic lower auxiliary note (circled in blue), while bar 2 has an example of a chromatic passing note (circled in red).

Beethoven, Sonata in G minor, Op. 49 No.1 (Rondo)

Audio 14.2

In this extract bars 3 and 19 contain examples of chromatic passing notes, while bars 7, 11 and 15 feature chromatic appoggiaturas (circled in green).

Mozart, Sonata in C major, K545 (3rd mvt)

Audio 14.3

In this extract bar 3 has a series of diatonic appoggiaturas, while bar 4 includes a chromatic passing note.

Mozart, Sonata in B flat major, K333 (2nd mvt)

Chromatic passing notes

You are already familiar with diatonic passing notes both unaccented and accented. The chromatic passing note creates a semitone step between the harmony notes on either side. It may be unaccented or accented.

Listen to the following audio extracts to hear examples of chromatic passing notes which are circled on the scores.

Audio 14.4a

The circled notes show a series of chromatic passing notes in a descending profile.

Haydn, Sonata in E flat major, Hob XVI:52 (3rd mvt)

Audio 14.4b

Later in the same movement the chromatic passing notes appear in an ascending profile. Note in the penultimate bar, that both passing notes are accented, giving more drive to the line.

Audio 14.5

The chromatic passing notes in this extract are placed on strong beats in bars 2 and 4, giving a sense of forward impetus.

Mozart, Sonata in D major, K576 (3rd mvt)

Summary

- Chromatic passing notes always move by semitone steps
- Ascending chromatic passing notes normally use raised accidental signs
- Descending chromatic passing notes normally use lowered accidental signs

Chromatic auxiliary notes

Chromatic auxiliary notes are most commonly used as lower auxiliary creating a semitone step below the harmony note, whereas upper auxiliary notes are always diatonic.

Listen to the following audio extracts to hear examples of chromatic auxiliary notes that are circled on the scores.

Audio 14.6

This extract uses chromatic lower auxiliary notes in bars 2 and 3. Here they are placed on the accented part of beat 3 in both instances.

Mozart, Sonata in F major, K135 (1st mvt) adapted

Audio 14.7

The first 4 bars of this extract are written in sequence where lower auxiliary notes decorate the treble line. Note the auxiliary notes in bars 2 and 3 are chromatic, whilst the auxiliary notes in bars 1 and 4 are diatonic - already being semitone steps. A further chromatic lower auxiliary note decorates the bass part of bars 5-8.

Mozart, Sonata in G major, K283 (3rd mvt)

Audio 14.8

In this extract the chromatic lower auxiliary notes fall on the unaccented part of the beat.

Beethoven, Bagatelle in A minor No.25 *Fur Elise*

Summary

- Chromatic auxiliary notes always move by semitone steps
- Chromatic auxiliary notes are always **lower** auxiliary
- Chromatic auxiliary notes may be unaccented or accented

Appoggiaturas

The word appoggiatura translates as a leaning note and for this reason it is always placed on a strong beat or strong part of any beat. An appoggiatura, being a dissonant note, has much in common with both a suspension and an accented passing note, but is freer in its approach, not needing a preparation. An appoggiatura is always struck and resolves by step to a harmony note. An appoggiatura that resolves downward is diatonic, whereas an appoggiatura that resolves upwards is normally a rising semitone step and therefore is often chromatic.

The next three audios contain examples of appoggiaturas (circled in green on the scores). As you listen, be aware that the appoggiatura is dissonant while it temporarily displaces the harmony note.

Audio 14.9

Listen again to an extract from earlier in the chapter and focus now on bar 3. The circled appoggiaturas in this instance are all diatonic and resolve downwards by step to harmony notes. Each of these appoggiaturas is approached by a leap as no preparation is needed.

Audio 14.10

As you listen to Audio 14.10 notice that in bars 4 and 5 the appoggiaturas are written as small print notes while in bars 6 and 7, they are fully written out.

- Appoggiaturas may appear as small print notes (emphasising their decorative quality)
- Appoggiaturas are diatonic when resolving downwards
- Appoggiaturas are chromatic when resolving upwards to form a rising semitone step
- Appoggiaturas need no preparation and may be approached by leap, by step or from a repeated note.

Audio 14.11

Listen carefully to this extract and read the commentary that follows below.

In this extract all the examples of appoggiaturas are highlighted. Those in bars 3 – 6 are all chromatic and rising. Those in bars 8 and 10 are all diatonic and falling. Look at the variety of approaches – the first 3 appoggiaturas are approached by leap. In bar 6 the approach is by step and finally in bars 8 and 10 the approach is from a repeated note. Because of the large degree of freedom in approaching an appoggiatura, an alternative analysis is often possible, for example, the F sharp in bar 6 may equally be described as a chromatic passing note. Let's examine bar 8 – are we dealing here with an appoggiatura or a suspension? The answer is clear! The small print notation means that the labelling is always an appoggiatura. However, if it had been written using full size notation, one might wonder could it be explained as a suspension because of the repeated pitches? This is less likely as a suspension is commonly tied.

Summary

- An appoggiatura is always accented occupying either a whole accented beat or an accented part of a beat
- The approach to an appoggiatura has complete freedom
- An appoggiatura always resolves by step to a harmony note
- A falling appoggiatura is always diatonic
- A chromatic appoggiatura is always a rising semitone
- An appoggiatura may be written as a full size or small print note
- Appoggiaturas may also appear as a triple decoration especially at cadential points
- All types of melodic decoration may be used in pairs moving in 3rds (10ths) and 6ths

Listen to the following group of audios where double and triple decorations are highlighted on the scores.

Audio 14.12

In bar 2 of this extract right and left hands move in parallel 10ths featuring both chromatic auxiliary notes and chromatic passing notes.

Mozart, Sonata in C major, K330 (1st mvt)

Audio 14.13

Bars 2 and 4 of this extract feature chromatic auxiliary notes moving in parallel 3rds.

Mozart, Sonata in D major, K284 (2nd mvt)

The cadence in bar 8 is decorated with **Ic – V**. The **Ic** may also be interpreted as a double appoggiatura to chord **V**.

Audio 14.14

Bars 2 and 4 of this extract feature double appoggiaturas moving in 3rds.

Mozart, Sonata in C major, K330 (3rd mvt)

Audio 14.15

The final bar of this extract features a triple appoggiatura at the cadence point in F major. Note the varied approaches to the appoggiaturas.

Mozart, Sonata in F major, K533 (2nd mvt)

Exercise 14.1/ Audio 14.16

As you listen while following the score, identify each type of circled decoration.

Mozart, Sonata in C major, K330 (3rd mvt)

Bar 4 ______________ Bar 6 ______________

Bar 11 ______________ Bar 15 ______________

Bar 17 ______________ Bar 19 ______________

Exercise 14.2/ Audio 14.17

(a) Circle the 4 chromatic decorative elements in the first 2 bars of this C minor extract. The type of each chromatic note is ______________.

(b) Identify the type of decoration on the first beat of bar 4 ____________.

Allegro

Mozart, Sonata in C minor, K457 (3rd mvt)

Exercise 14.3/ Audio 14.18

Listen carefully to the following extract and focus particularly on the areas highlighted in blue. Fully describe the type of decoration used in each instance.

Mozart, Sonata in C major, K330 (2nd mvt)

Bar 2 ________________

Bar 7 ________________

Bar 8 ________________

Bar 10 ________________

Bar 14 ________________

Bar 16 ________________

Bar 18 ________________

Occasionally, two decorative notes may follow one another before reaching a resolution as seen in the following 2 short extracts.

Audio 14.19

Listen to this extract, focus on bar 5 and read the commentary below.

Mozart, Sonata in G major, K283 (3rd mvt)

Bar 5 is essentially a chord of A minor with the G sharp and B both being decorative around the harmony note A. The G sharp functions as a lower auxiliary while B functions as an upper auxiliary – one follows the other and both resolve on the fourth semiquaver A. The one resolution suffices for both.

Audio 14.20

Here is another example of two decorative notes following one another before resolving.

Mozart, Sonata in C major, K545 (3rd mvt)

In the treble of bar 1 the lower auxiliary D sharp is followed by the upper auxiliary F with both resolving on the harmony note E. This figure is repeated in bar 2 and occurs again in the bass part of bars 3 and 4.

Let us study a melody incorporating some chromatic decoration.

Step 1:

Listen carefully to the contour of the melody and identify any obvious decorative notes.

Audio 14.21

Bar 1: The quaver A sharp is best treated as a chromatic lower auxiliary note.

Bar 2: The quavers G sharp and A sharp suggest obvious chromatic passing notes.

Bar 3 can be reduced to this framework which makes clear the best notes to harmonise. This

points to F sharp and D sharp being decorative, i.e., a passing note followed by an appoggiatura /chromatic lower auxiliary note with both resolving to the harmony note E. The quaver B on the 4th beat is an appoggiatura which rises by semitone to the harmony note C.

Bar 4: C sharp is an obvious chromatic passing note/appoggiatura to D, while the crotchet F sharp on the 3rd beat leans into the final G forming an appoggiatura.

Step 2:

Let us choose a possible harmonisation based on the framework discussed and add the bass line.

The suggested chording is quite simple to allow the chromaticism to shine through.

Audio 14.22

Listen to the outline of the chording with treble and bass parts.

Step 3:
Adding alto and tenor voices completes the 4-part harmonisation. Of particular note is the triple decoration at the final cadence.

Audio 14.23

Now listen to the final step of the harmonisation. Although the melody contains much decorative detail, the uncomplicated harmonisation underpins and supports the simple underlying framework.

Exercise 14.4

Sing or play each melody to identify any obvious chromatic decoration. Harmonise by adding a bass line. Then complete a 4-part harmonisation with alto and tenor parts.

(a)

(b)

(c)

(d)

CHAPTER 15

FURTHER CHROMATIC CHORDS Part 1
The Neapolitan 6th

The Neapolitan 6th chord is predominantly found in association with chord **V** as a colourful approach chord adding depth and intensity to the harmony, typically at cadential points. The Neapolitan 6th chord provides a rather dark brooding quality.

Audio 15.1a/b

Listen to the following audio extracts while studying the scores. The highlighted areas pinpoint examples of the Neapolitan 6th chord.

(a)

Haydn, Sonata in C minor, Hob XVI:20

(b)

Haydn, String Quartet, Op.17 No.1 (3rd mvt)

Forming the Neapolitan 6th

The Neapolitan 6th chord is normally found in the minor key. It is a chromatically altered version of the supertonic chord. Study the examples below in A minor.

ii°

Chord **ii** is diminished.

♭ii

The root of chord **ii** is flattened to become a major triad.

♭iib

This major triad is arranged in first inversion to form the Neapolitan 6th chord.

The 6th refers to the figured bass, indicating a first inversion.

Roman numerals may use either of the following when describing Neapolitan 6th chords: **♭iib** or **N6**

Figured bass uses the following depending on the key signature: **♭6** or **♮6**

For convenience in text, **N6** will be used when referring to the Neapolitan 6th chord.

The resolution of the N6 chord is to **V** or **ic-V**.

In 4-part writing the third of the chord (the bass note) is always doubled as seen in the examples below in A minor.

Comparing the familiar progression **iib – V** in the first example with the chromatically altered form of **N6 – V** notice that only one note has changed (circled). Instead of the diminished **iib** we hear a chord of B flat major.

Audio 15.2

Listen and compare the effect of each of the progressions above noting the rich effect created by the N6 chord.

Here are examples of perfect cadences approached by the N6 chord in A minor.

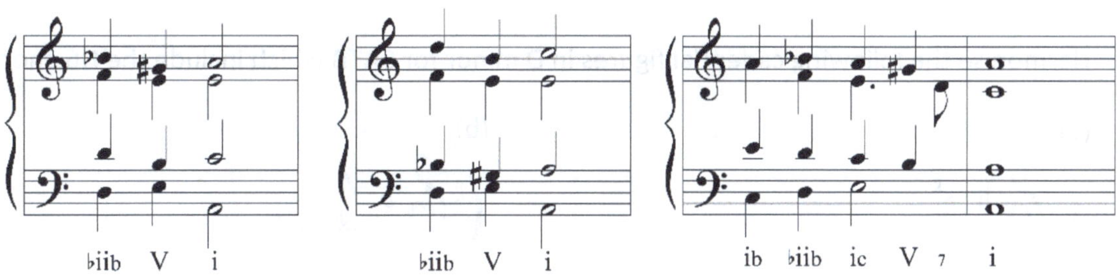

Audio 15.3

Listen to the three short cadential figures above.

The next examples show some possible approaches to an imperfect cadence using the N6 chord.

The N6 resolves to **V7d**.

The N6 resolves through **ic** to **V**

Audio 15.4

Listen to the above progressions with the N6 chord giving a colourful lead into an imperfect cadence.

The N6 chord is a major chord a semitone above the tonic. It is used in 1st inversion

Exercise 15.1

Harmonise the following cadential figures in D minor for SATB which include the N6 chord.

(a)

(b)

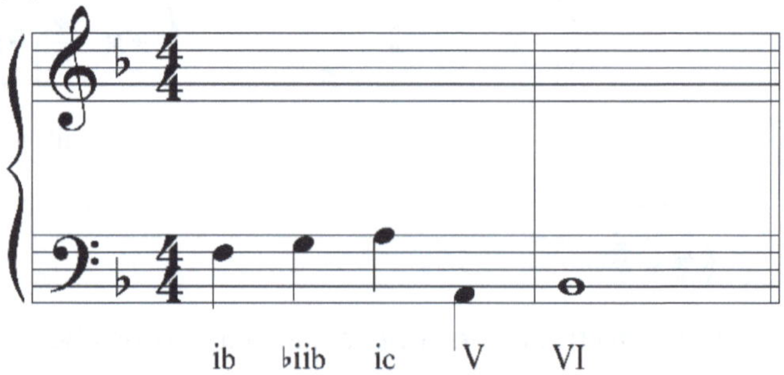

(c)

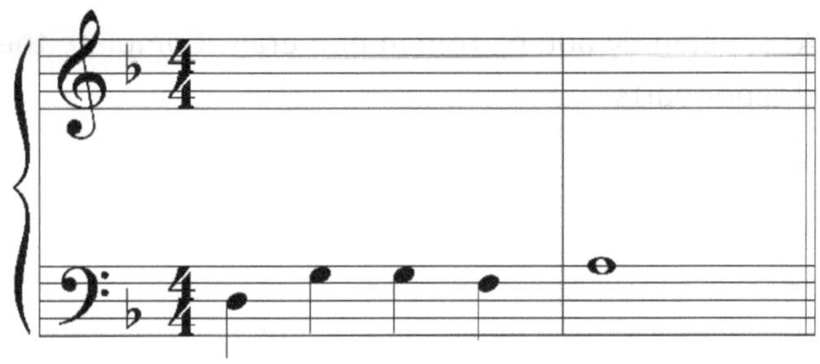

i ♭iib V7d ib V

Exercise 15.2

Write the following progressions for SATB in E minor and C minor respectively.

(a)

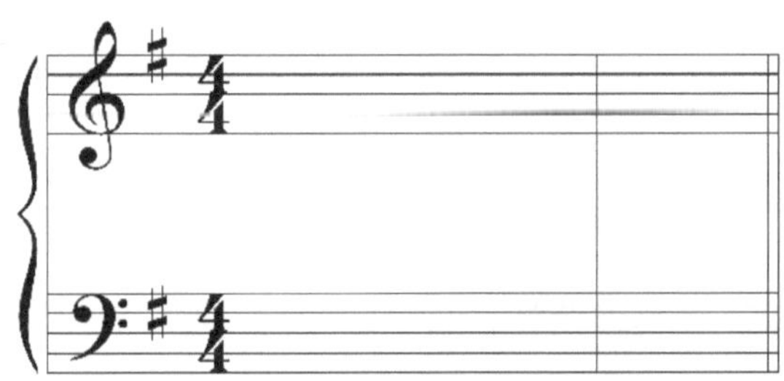

i ♭iib ic V i

(b)

VI ♭iib ic V i

(c)

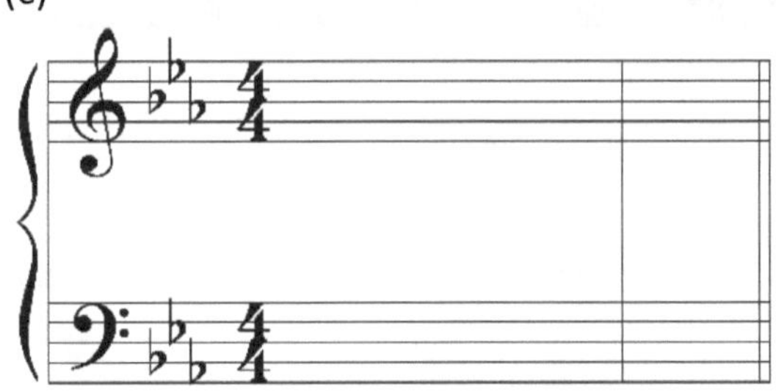

ib ♭iib V7d ib V

(d)

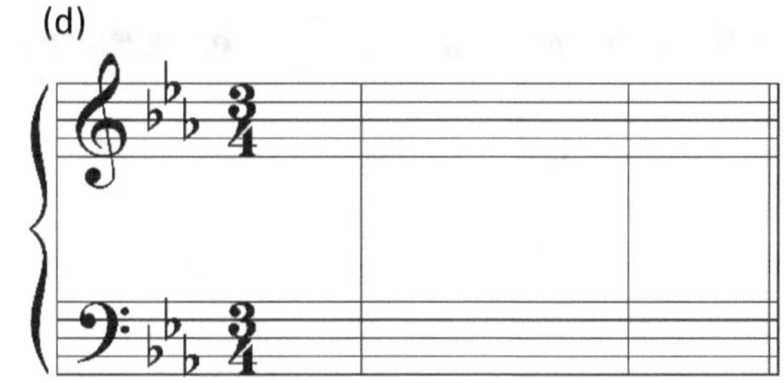

i ♭iib V 7 VI

Exercise 15.3

Realise the following figured bass lines for SATB. Begin by adding roman numerals. Complete the soprano melody first, then finally add alto and tenor parts.

(a)

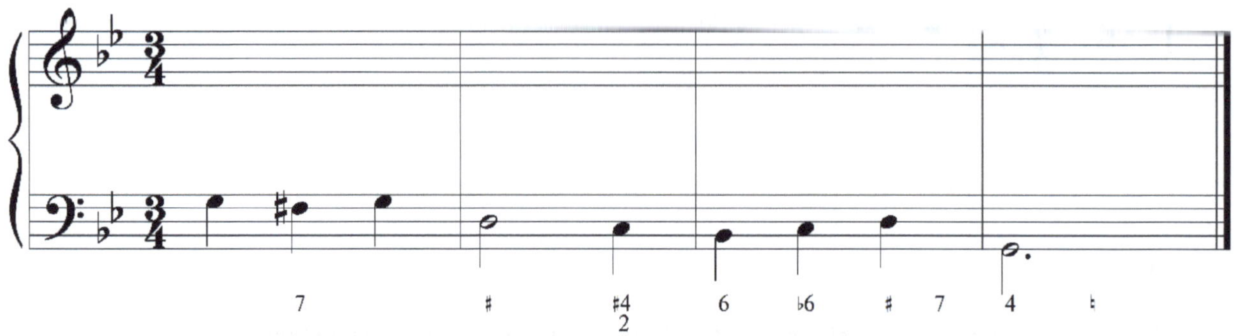

(b)

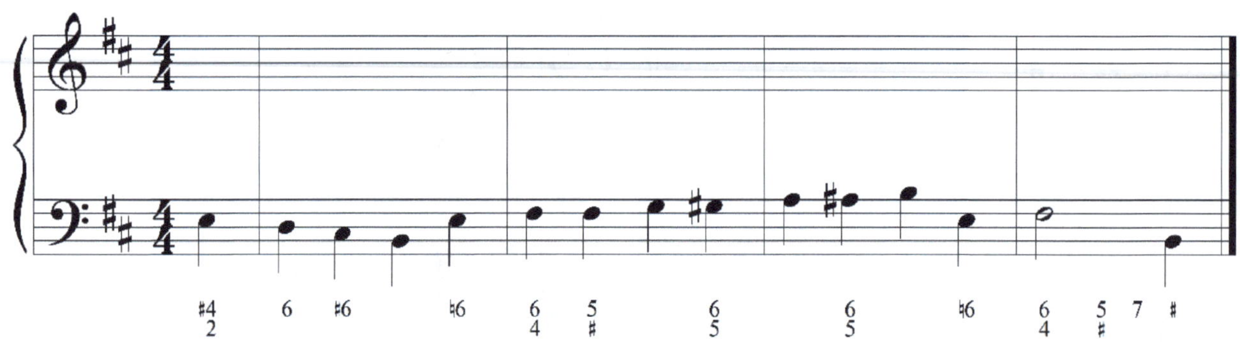

A further enhancement, in the form of a chromatic semitone step, may be inserted in the bass between the N6 chord and its resolution to chord **V**. This intensifies the overall harmonic effect.

This added chromatic note is effectively harmonised by a diminished 7th chord as **vii7** of **V**.

To this rising bass line, a soprano of ***m r d t l*** works effectively in a scalic contrary motion shape.

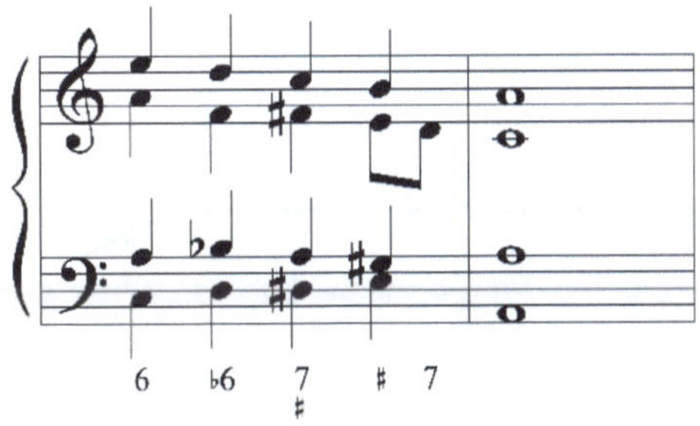

Alto and tenor parts complete the 4-part harmonisation.

Audio 15.5

Compare both fragments above, first you hear the contrary motion of the outer lines followed by the full rich 4-part harmonisation.

Exercise 15.4

Complete the following idioms for SATB.

(a)

(b)

(c)

Summary

- N6 is a chromatically altered form of the supertonic triad usually reserved for the minor key
- N6 is a major chord a semitone above the tonic - used in 1st inversion
- Double the 3rd of the chord
- N6 resolves to chord **V** or **ic-V**
- N6 may move through a diminished 7th chord before resolving to chord **V** or **ic-V**
- The melodic idiom ***m r d t l*** offers an opportunity to use this colourful harmonic progression: **i (or ib), N6, vii7/V, V, i.**

Exercise 15.5/ Audio 15.6 a/b/c

Listen to the following audio extracts in conjunction with the printed scores.
Begin by identifying the key of each extract and make a note of the N6 chord in the space provided.
Then circle all instances of the N6 chord.

Remember the N6 is a major chord a semitone above the tonic.

(a) Key: __________ N6 chord: _________

Beethoven, Sonata. Op.31 No.2 (1st mvt)

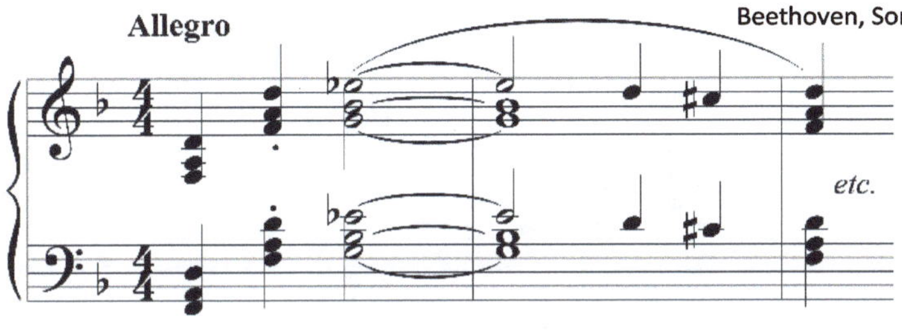

(b) Key: __________ N6 chord: _________

Mozart, Concerto in A, K488 (2nd mvt.)

(c) Key: __________ N6 chord: _________

Chopin, Nocturne Op.55 No.1

Exercise 15.6/ Audio 15.7 a/b

Listen to the following audio extracts in conjunction with the printed scores.
Analyse the specified chords by using roman numerals.

(a)

J.S. Bach, Chorale *Ach Gott vom Himmel*

Bar 2: beat 2 _____, beat 3 _____, beat 4 _____.

Bar 3: beat 1 _____, beat 2 _____, beat 3 _____, beat 4 _____.

Bar 4: beat 1 _____.

(b)

Schubert, *Der Muller und der Bach* (D.795)

Bar 7: _____. Bar 8: _____. Bar 9: _____. Bar 10: _____.

Bar 15: _____. Bar 16: _____. Bar 17: _____. Bar 18: _____.

CHAPTER 16

FURTHER CHROMATIC CHORDS Part 2
The Augmented 6th chord

The augmented 6th chord provides another chromatic and striking approach to chord **V** adding brightness and intensity to the harmony. It is common in both major and minor keys.

Audio 16.1

Listen to the following audio extracts while studying the scores. The highlighted areas pinpoint examples of the Augmented 6th chord in the context of (a) a piano sonata by Mozart and (b) a Beethoven symphony.

(a)

Mozart, Sonata in E flat, K 282 (2nd mvt)

(b)

Beethoven, Symphony No.5, C minor (1st mvt)

Two essential notes form the basis of the Augmented 6th chord – the flattened 6th and the raised 4th of the scale.

In the key of C major, by chromatically altering two notes, namely, flattening the 6th and raising the 4th, the interval of an augmented 6th is created - hence the name given to the chord.

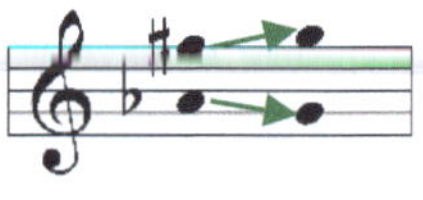

Each note resolves by pushing outward in semitone steps i.e., the raised 4th rising to the 5th and the flattened 6th falling to the 5th.

The augmented 6th chord has three variants known as the Italian 6th, the German 6th and the French 6th which may be abbreviated as follows: It6th, Ger6th, and Fr6th.

For convenience, in text, the Augmented 6th chord will be referred to as Aug6.

Italian 6th

You are familiar with the progression **IVb – V.** In a major key, if we chromatically alter 2 notes, the It6th is formed.
Note the necessary doubling i.e., the 5th of the chord is doubled.

Always avoid doubling chromatically altered notes

 Audio 16.2

Listen to both examples above noting the more colourful Aug6 chord.

Here is **ivb – V** in C minor followed by the chromatic alteration to create the Aug6 chord. When using the Aug6 in a minor key, notice only one note is chromatically altered.

Audio 16.3

Listen to both examples above for comparison.

When writing for SATB, as heard in the preceding examples, an effective arrangement is to place the augmented 6th interval between the bass and soprano parts.

The It6th chord resolves to **V** or **Ic – V**.

Note the figured bass.

Audio 16.4

Listen to the C major examples above to hear both resolutions.

Next are some typical approaches to the It6th chord.

Audio 16.5

Listen to each of the progressions above.

- It6th chords may resolve to **V** or **Ic – V**
- Double the 3rd from the bass

Exercise 16.1

Add SAT to the given bass progressions which include the It6th chord.

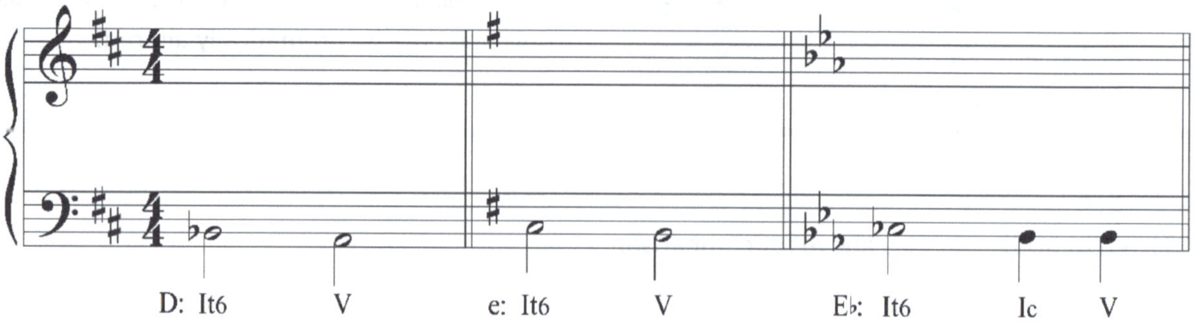

Exercise 16.2

Write the following progressions for SATB in the given keys.

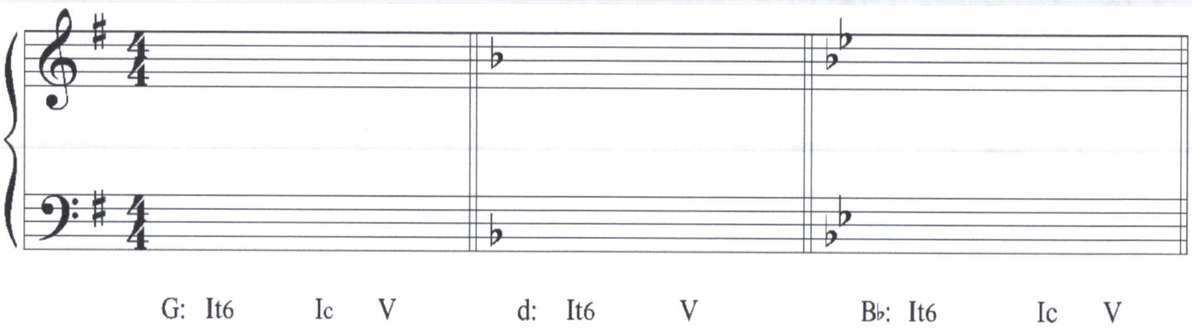

Exercise 16.3

Complete parts for SAT according to the given figured bass.

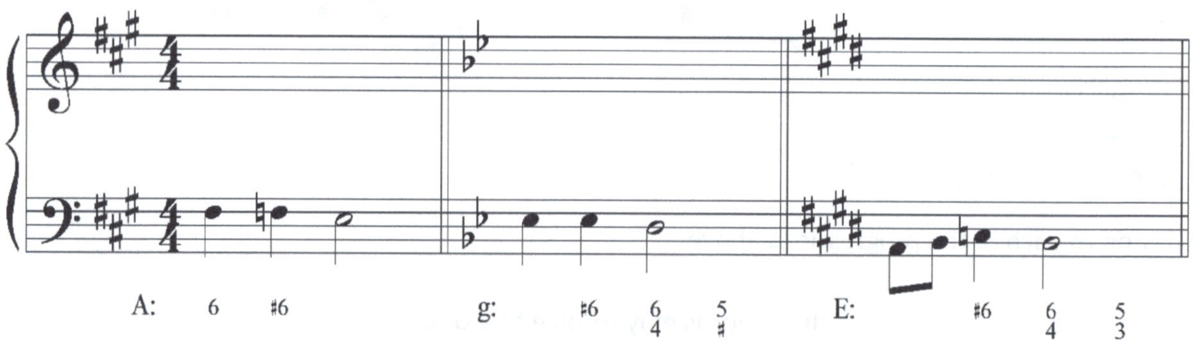

As mentioned earlier, there are three variants of the Aug6 chord, the distinguishing feature being the added notes.

Italian 6th

You are already familiar with this Aug6 chord, it is the type most used. These three notes are present in all variants.

German 6th

The added note is a perfect 5th above the bass of the chord. As there are four notes present no doubling is needed when writing for SATB.

French 6th

The added note is an augmented 4th above the bass of the chord. Again, no doubling is required when writing for SATB.

The augmented 6th interval will always resolve outward by semitone steps in all variants.

Italian

German

French

Audio 16.6

Compare the 3 examples above. You will hear each Aug6 as a broken chord to easily distinguish the different pitches present in each type.

German 6th

Audio 16.7

Listen to the following short extract in G minor while studying the score. The extract includes an example of the Ger6th chord which is highlighted in bar 2. It resolves to **V** in the following bar. First, look at the reduction of the progression included here.

Mozart, Sonata in B flat, K 333 (3rd mvt)

Audio 16.8

Listen to this extract in A flat major for voice and piano. The Ger6th chord is highlighted in bar 8; it resolves through **Ic** to **V7** in the following bar. A reduction of the progression is included.

Beethoven, 'In Questa Tomba Oscura' WoO 133

Here is the progression of the Ger6th in C major. When writing specifically for SATB, particular care must be taken with the voice leading.

The resolution of the augmented 6th interval moves as expected. Let's investigate how the other voices progress.

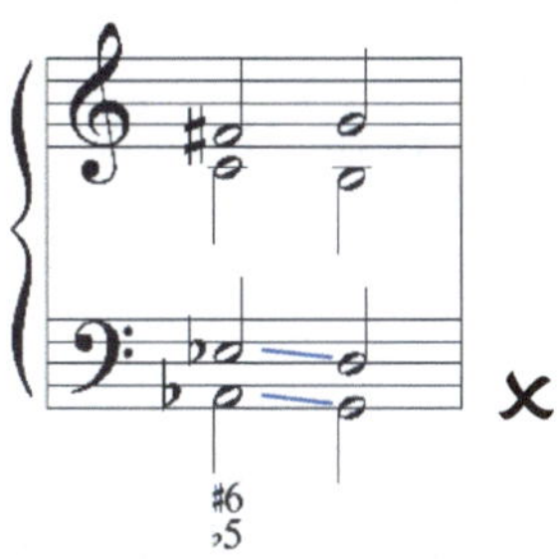

The parallel 5^{ths} between the tenor and bass parts create an obvious difficulty.

The solution is to resolve via **Ic** – **V**.

In the minor key we see that the resolution of the Ger6th requires the same solution – progressing through **ic** to **V**.

Audio 16.9

Listen to the two previous examples to hear the Ger6th resolving to **Ic** – **V** in major and minor keys.

- Ger6th chords resolve to **V**, but when writing for SATB it is necessary to resolve through **Ic** to **V**
- All 4 pitches should be present requiring no doubling
- The approach chords are the same as for the It6th

Exercise 16.4

Add SAT to the given bass progressions which include the Ger6th chord.

Exercise 16.5

Complete parts for SAT according to the given figured bass.

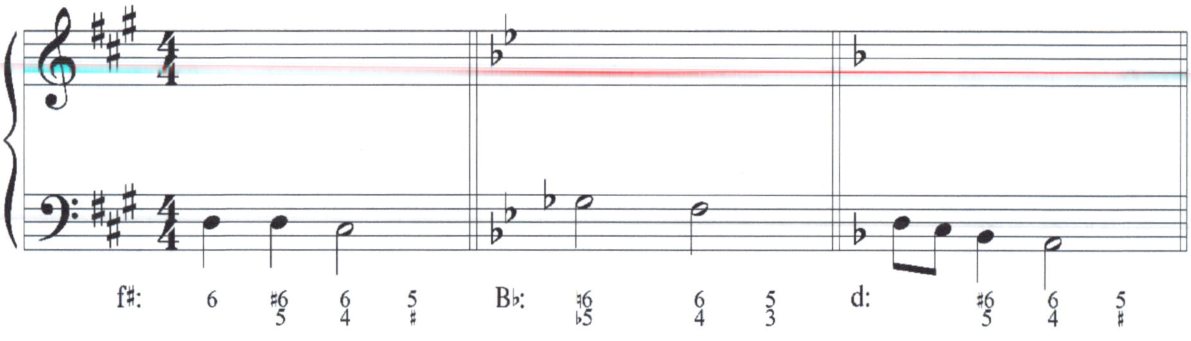

More about the German 6th

In isolation, the Ger6th chord sounds the same as a dominant 7th chord, the difference being in the spelling of one note.

When the F sharp pitch (the augmented 6th interval) is enharmonically changed to G flat (minor 7th interval) the chord now functions as a dominant 7th in a different key and consequently has quite a different resolution.

Audio 16.10

As you listen compare the two progressions. In the case of the Ger6th there is an anticipatory quality to resolve to chord **V** or **Ic** – **V** as the extremes of the chord push outward semitonally. Whereas, in the case of the dominant 7th, the minor 7th interval resolves inwards to a completely new tonality. This shows potential for future exploration into more advanced modulation.

French 6th

Audio 16.11

Listen to the following piano extract in A minor. Focus on bar 11 where the Fr6th is highlighted – notice the sound has a 'clustered' effect. Included is a reduction of the progression.

Brahms, *Variations on a theme by Paganini* Op. 35

This example in C major shows the resolution of the augmented 6th interval moving as expected while the remaining voices progress smoothly to chord **V**.

The resolution may also move through **Ic** to **V**.

The progression of the Fr6th is the same in the minor key.

Audio 16.12

Listen to the previous three examples to hear the Fr6th resolving in both major and minor keys.

- Fr6th chords may resolve to **V** or **Ic** - **V**
- All 4 pitches should be present requiring no doubling
- The approach chords are the same as for the It6th and Ger6th chords

As a general rule of thumb chromatic chords are best approached smoothly

Exercise 16.6

(a) Add SAT to the given bass progressions which include the Fr6th chord.

(b) Add SAT according to the given figured bass.

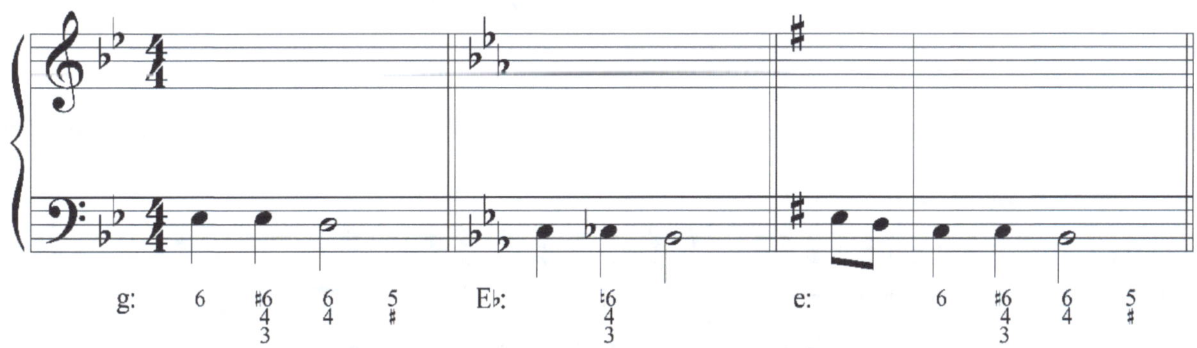

Exercise 16.7

Harmonise the given soprano fragments to include an Aug6 chord. Make use of each of the three variants. When complete add the figured bass.

Exercise 16.8/ Audio 16.13a/b/c

Study the score while listening to each extract. Identify the key of the passage (it may not always be in the tonic key). Locate an Aug6 chord. Name the type as either It6th, Ger6th or Fr6th. State whether the resolution is to chord **V** or **Ic – V**.

(a)

Beethoven, *Adelaide* Op. 46

An Aug6 chord occurs in bar _____, beat(s) _____.

The type of this Aug6 chord is __________.

The resolution is to chord _____.

(b)

An Aug6 chord occurs in bar _____, beat(s) _____.

The type of this Aug6 chord is _________.

The resolution is to chord _____.

(c)

Schubert, *'Der Wegweiser'* No.20, Wintereisse

An Aug6 chord occurs in bar _____, beat(s) _____.

The type of this Aug6 chord is _________.

The resolution is to chord _____.

Spotting opportunities to use Aug6 chords in a bass line

Let us study the following bass line and consider a likely harmonisation.

Bar 4 offers an opportunity approaching the cadence to add Aug6 colouring. The aim is to include the flattened 6th note (E flat) in the bass line.

IVb Aug6 Ic V

This is easily achieved by chromatically altering **IVb** to include a move from E to E flat on beat 2.

When creating the soprano line, it can be useful to sketch in the preferred shaping in bar 4 (i.e. the raised 4th) and craft the melody line towards that point.

Now to complete the melody line.

The final step is to complete parts for the inner voices. The choice will emerge as to which type of Aug6 chord to use in bar 4. We have opted for the Ger6th, but the It6th and Fr6th types would be equally effective. The completed harmonisation below adds some extra interest in the detail of the alto line in bar 2 and includes the figured bass.

Audio 16.14

First you will hear the soprano and bass parts followed by the full 4-part harmonisation.

Exercise 16.9

Study the bass lines in the following exercises and adjust/interpret to include an example of an Aug6 chord at a suitable point. For practice use a different type in each exercise. Add SAT.

(a)

(b)

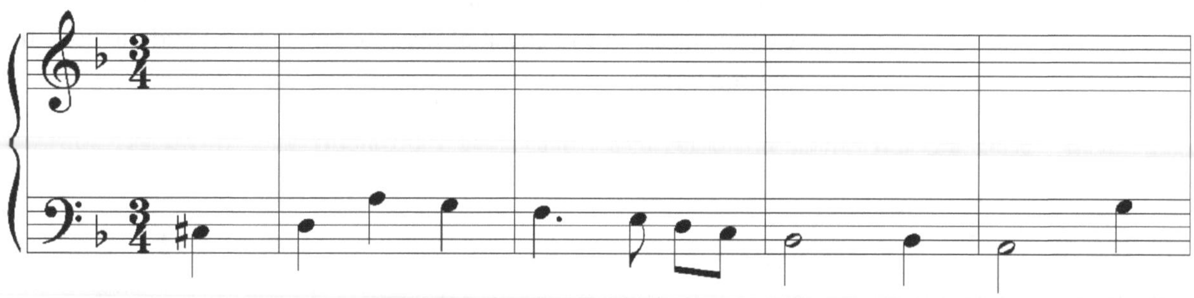

(c)

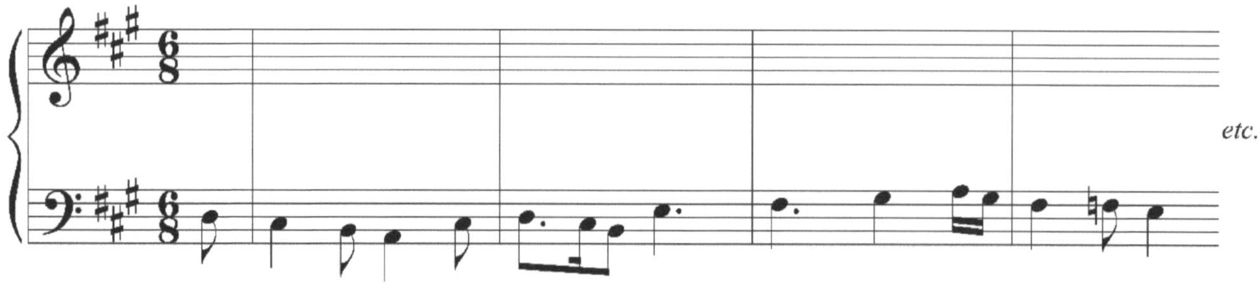

Harmonising chromaticism in a melody line

When approaching the harmonisation of a melody it may be useful to identify certain melodic features which may offer clues to an effective harmonisation.

Here is a summary of some typical melodic features to consider.

- The raised 4th rising to the 5th of the scale (***fi* – *s*, *ri* - *m***) suggests a number of strong possibilities:
    1) A modulation to the dominant key with **V – I**
    2) A secondary dominant chord as **V** of **V**
    3) A diminished 7th chord as **vii7** of **V**
    4) An augmented 6th chord with its resolution
- Shorter note values in semitone steps suggest:
    1) Chromatic auxiliary notes
    2) Chromatic passing notes
- A strong to weak rhythm at a cadential point is often decorative, consider the following:
    1) Cadential 2nd inversion: **Ic – V**
    2) Suspension
    3) Appoggiatura

As we sing and study this melody let us see what points from above may be relevant in supporting a strong harmonisation.

There are three instances of the raised 4th to the 5th (***fi* – *s***) in bar 3-4, bar 5-6 and bar 7.

There are three instances of quaver movement involving chromatic semitone steps in bar 3 and bars 5-6.

The melody ends with a strong to weak rhythm suggesting an appoggiatura.

Let us divide up the melody into 2-bar segments and consider some appropriate possibilities for harmonisation.

Bars 1 and 2

This rising scalic bass line uses two simple idiomatic progressions.

An alternative bass line forms a strong contrary motion shape to the melody line. The use of the diminished 7th in bar 2 draws in some chromatic colouring.

Bars 3 and 4

In all instances the soprano G sharp quaver is treated as a chromatic lower auxiliary note.

Both the previous and this harmonisation show a clear-cut modulation to the dominant key confirmed by the cadence.

Bars 3 and 4 continued

With the addition of a semitone step in the bass (F sharp on beat 2) between chords **IV** and **V** an opportunity for the diminished 7th chord as **vii7** of **V** is created.

The ***fi* – *s*** in the soprano creates an ideal opportunity to heighten the colour by using the Aug6 chord. Any variant may be chosen.

Bars 5 and 6 including the upbeat

This and the following option both use simple diatonic harmony (mostly tonic/dominant), while recognising the chromatic auxiliary notes in the quaver rhythm.

Here the harmony is more colourful with the use of the diminished 7th as **vii7** of **vi** on the upbeat. The downbeat of bar 6 introduces another chromaticism in the form of a secondary dominant chord as **V** of **IV**.

Bars 7 and 8

A secondary dominant is used to harmonise the B natural in the soprano as **V** of **V**. The soprano G in the final bar is best treated as an appoggiatura. (There may also be an opportunity for further appoggiaturas in the inner voices).

Alternatively, the B natural can also be treated as an appoggiatura, complimenting the appoggiatura in the final bar.

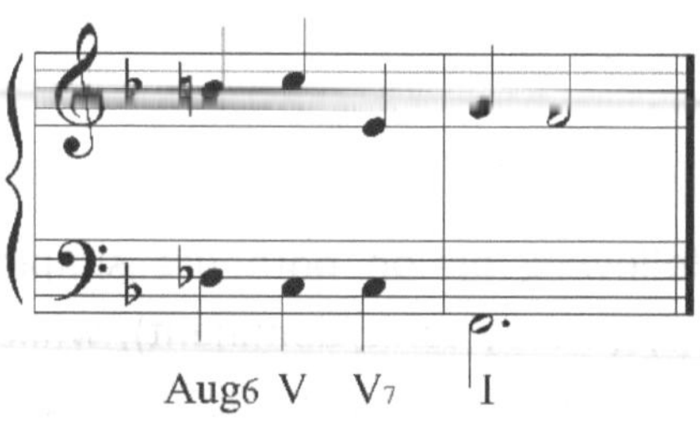

This final harmonisation maximises the chromatic content by using the Aug6 chord (any variant may be chosen).

In summing up, whilst there is a varied selection of available harmonisations, below are two contrasting solutions.

(a)

(b)

Audio 16.15

Listen to both harmonisations while following the scores. Compare the simple yet effective first solution of (a) with the more chromatic treatment offered in (b).

Exercise 16.10

Harmonise each melody looking for suitable opportunities to use the various chromatic features studied to date.

(a)

(b)

(c)

(d)

CHAPTER 17

HARMONIC ANALYSIS 3

These analysis extracts include secondary 7th, secondary dominant, chromatic chords and modulation together with decorative elements.

The extracts are taken from Baroque, Classical and early Romantic literature. While some extracts are from the beginning of a piece or movement, others are not. For the sake of simplicity in bar numbering all extracts will be taken as beginning with bar 1.

You may listen to each audio extract as often as you wish.

Exercise 17.1 Audio 17.1

Listen as you study the opening bars from the second movement of Beethoven's piano sonata Op. 14, No. 2. Then answer the questions that follow.

(i) Name the key to which the music has modulated by the end of the extract. ____________

(ii) Mark a possible pivot chord to approach the new key. (contd.)

(iii) Name the type of cadence in bar 4 ____________ and in bar 8 ____________.

(iv) Which of these terms correctly describes the chromatic chord on the 4th beat of bar 3?

secondary 7th, secondary dominant, diminished 7th. ________________

What is its relationship to the chord on the 1st beat of bar 4? _________________________

(v) Using roman numerals and writing below the stave, analyse the harmonies in the shaded area in bars 7 and 8.

Exercise 17.2 Audio 17.2

The following extract is from the opening of the 3rd movement of Mozart's Fantasia K.475. Listen while you study the score to answer the questions in relation to it.

(i) Name the tonic key ________and the type of cadence reached at bar 4. ______________

(ii) Circle the three decorative notes in the treble of bar 3.

(iii) Are your circled notes best described as auxiliary notes or appoggiaturas? ______________

(iv) Draw a box around a chord in bar 3 that functions as a secondary dominant.

(v) In bars 5 – 8 circle an example of a rising chromatic appoggiatura and its resolution.

(vi) How is the final perfect cadence decorated? ______________________________________

Exercise 17.3 Audio 17.3

Listen to the opening bars of Mozart's Motet *Ave Verum Corpus* K.618. Then answer the questions that follow.

(i) Name the tonic key. ________

(ii) Name the type of cadence reached at bar 4 ___________ and at bar 8 ____________.

(iii) In bars 9 – 16 the music modulates to the key of ___________ and ends with a _____________ cadence.

(iv) Explain the circled notes in bar 4. ________________

(v) What type of chord is formed on the first crotchet of bar 12 _____________ and how does this chord relate to the chord that follows? ______________________

(vi) Circle 2 examples of suspension in the last 4-bar phrase.

(vii) Using roman numerals, name the chord highlighted on the last crotchet of bar 14. ______

Exercise 17.4 Audio 17.4

The short extract below is taken from Schubert's *Moment Musicale* Op.94, No.6. Listen carefully and answer the questions that follow.

(i) The section that immediately precedes the printed extract is in the key of E major. Has the first printed chord in this extract any relationship to the preceding key? ________________

(ii) The key is now established as A flat major; what type of cadence ends the phrase at bar 4? ____________. What type of cadence ends the extract? ______________

(iii) How is the final cadence of the extract decorated? ____________________

(iv) Circle an example of a 4 – 3 suspension.

(v) Analyse the harmonies in the shaded area. Write on the score below the stave.

Exercise 17.5a, b Audio 17.5a, b

The two extracts that follow are taken from the second movement of Mozart's Piano sonata in F K.280. Extract (a) is the opening 17 bars. Extract (b) is the concluding 4 bars of the movement.

(a)

(i) Name the tonic key. ___________. Name the new key in bars 9 – 17. ___________

(ii) Locate and circle a triple suspension/appoggiatura.

(iii) Fully explain the harmony in bar 13 in relation to the change of key. ___________

(iv) In which bar is there an example of a chromatic diminished 7th in the change of key? ____

(v) Circle one of the figured basses below that relates to the dominant 7th chord in bar 16.

7	6	4	4
	5	3	2

(b)

These final 4 bars are in the tonic key. The shaded areas highlight chromatic colouring with relevant resolutions. Using roman numerals and writing on the score below the stave, analyse the harmonies in these areas.

Exercise 17.6 Audio 17.6

Listen to the opening section of the 2nd movement from Haydn's String quartet in G minor Op. 74 No. 3. With the aid of the score, answer the questions that follow.

(i) Add roman numerals below the cello line to analyse the harmonies in bars 1 – 4.

(ii) Which of the bars you have analysed uses a secondary 7th chord? Bar:____.

(iii) Bars 5 – 8 are in the dominant key with some chromatic colouring. Describe the function of the chords in bar 5 beat 3 ______________ and throughout bar 8 _________________.

(iv) Name the type of decorative note circled in bar 7 __________ and bar 9 ___________.

(v) Include figured bass below the cello line in the final bar.

Exercise 17.7 Audio 17.7

Listen to a variation from the 3rd movement of Mozart's piano sonata in D, K 284. There are two repeated sections, answer the questions that follow in relation to each.

Section 1:

(i) Name the tonic key. __________ Name the key at the end of the first section. __________

(ii) Identify the highlighted chord on the last beat of bar 3. __________. How and where does this chord resolve? ____________________

(iii) In the light of the key change confirmed in bars 7 and 8, what is the function of the harmony throughout bar 6? ______________

Section 2:

(iv) Circle an example of a chromatic diminished 7th chord with its resolution.

(v) Which bar has a sequence of $\substack{6\\3}$ chords? Bar: ____

(vi) Draw a box around an example of an Italian augmented 6th chord.

Exercise 17.8 Audio 17.8

This extract is part of a Bagatelle by Beethoven Op. 33, No. 4. Listen while studying the score to complete the sentences and questions that follow.

(i) The overall key of this section is A minor; however, there is brief colouring of two other keys in the first four bars, namely: ____________ and ___________

(ii) The key of A minor is first confirmed by a _________ cadence reached in bar ___.

(iii) Identify the harmony in the shaded area in relation to A minor. _____________

(iv) Locate an example of a secondary 7th chord. Bar ___ beat ___

(v) Locate an example of a secondary dominant chord. Bar ___ beat ___

(vi) Locate and circle an example of a German augmented 6th chord.

Exercise 17.9 Audio 17.9

Listen to the opening of Beethoven's string quartet in D, Op. 18, No.3. Answer the questions below with the aid of the score.

(i) Analyse the harmonies by writing the roman numerals below the stave for bars 3 – 8.

(ii) Circle a suspension in the first violin part in bar 3.

(iii) Circle an appoggiatura in the first violin part in bar 5.

(iv) Bars 9 and 10 are a decorated form of the tonic chord; circle the decorative notes and describe the type used. ________________

(v) The final 3 bars of the extract suggest a colouring of E minor, with this in mind, describe the harmony in bar 16. ________________

(vi) Circle a chromatic auxiliary note in bar 17.

Exercise 17.10 Audio 17.10

This extract is from the 2nd movement of Haydn's string quartet in G minor Op. 74, No. 3. Listen to the music while studying the score to complete the sentences and questions below.

(i) The opening few bars in E minor are built on a tonic pedal; the key changes from the second half of bar 4 to the key of ___________. The dominant 7th chord on the 3rd beat of bar 4 is in __________ inversion. The new key is confirmed by a ___________ cadence reached at bar___. There is an augmented 6th chord in bar ___ beats______, its type is ____________ (Italian/German/French). It resolves in the next bar where the chords are ___ and ___.

(ii) In the second system identify one example of each of the following:

a chromatic auxiliary note (circle it and mark it A).

a chromatic passing note (circle it and mark it P).

Exercise 17.11 Audio 17.11

This extract is the opening of the 3rd movement from Haydn's string quartet in C, Op. 50, No. 2. Listen while studying the score, then answer the questions that follow.

The tonic key is established in the first 8 bars with some chromatic colouring:

(i) What is the function of the chord on the 3rd beat of bar 3? ________________

Name the resolution chords in bar 4. _____&_____

(ii) What is the function of the chord on the 2nd beat of bar 7? ________________

Name the resolution chord on the 3rd beat of bar 7. _____

(iii) Describe how the tonic chord in bar 8 is decorated. ____________________________

A new key is established in bars 9 -19, namely: _____________

(iv) What type of cadence ends the extract? _____________. Circle any decorative notes.

(v) In the 2nd system, locate an example of a diminished 7th chord (mark it x) and a secondary 7th chord (mark it y).

The [illegible] opening of [illegible]
[illegible] saying the [illegible]

[illegible]

[illegible] to [illegible] bars [illegible]

(i) What is the [illegible] of the [illegible] bars [illegible]

Name the resolution [illegible]

(ii) What are the [illegible] notes [illegible]

Name the resolution [illegible]

(iii) Describe how the tonic [illegible] 8 [illegible]

[illegible] new key is established [illegible] 9, namely [illegible]

(v) What type of cadence ends the [illegible] Circle any decorative notes

[illegible] type of [illegible] (use of [illegible]) [illegible]

[illegible] 7 [illegible]